KB140078

Marine
English

해 양 인 문 학 총 서

XIII

Marine English

Communicating through
Multimedia

Mae-Ran Park

Contents

Chapter 1. Oceans and Imagination / **7**

Chapter 2. Marine Weather Forecast / **19**

Chapter 3. Marine Tourism / **29**

Chapter 4. Oceans and Literature / **41**

Chapter 5. The World of Marine Bio-Resources / **63**

Chapter 6. Energy from the Ocean / **73**

Chapter 7. Marine Transportation / **85**

Chapter 8. Maritime History / **95**

Chapter 9. Water Sports and Sport Fishing / **107**

Chapter 10. Tastes of the Sea / **119**

Chapter 11. Restoring Marine Environment / **133**

Chapter 12. Saving the Future of the Sea / **145**

Appendix / **157**

Chapter 1. Oceans and Imagination

Chapter Forecast

- In this chapter, you will learn how to organize your speech into an effective opening, followed by a body, and a closing.
- You will practice how to share your opinion in a pair or small group, as well as in a whole class setting.
- You will learn practical tips to understand a short interview in a radio – by catching the key words and identifying main ideas.

Embark on a Journey Mapping the Ocean Cinema

- In pairs or groups, come up with the names of movies that are setting in the oceans or seas.
- Pick three movies that you think are best associated with the oceans or seas.
- Search on the web the names of oceans or seas the movies set in.
- Identify on the map the geographic location each movie set in.
- Discuss the reasons why you chose the three movies and why you think the movies are best associated with the oceans or seas. One person in your team will share a brief summary of your discussion with the whole class.
  - See **Speaking Tackle 1** (p. 8) for tips to organize your speech.

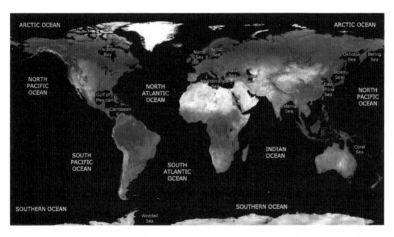

Figure 1 Oceans and Seas (https://www.seatemperature.org/oceans-seas)

Ocean Cinemas Scored Higher than 7/10 at IMDb
Information and synopsis taken from: www.imdb.com

The Abyss (1989)
PG-13/2h 25min/Adventure, Drama, Sci-Fi/Rate: 7.6/10

A civilian diving team is enlisted to search for a lost nuclear submarine and face danger while encountering an alien aquatic species.
Director: James Cameron
Writer: James Cameron
Stars:EdHarris,MaryElizabethMastrantonio,MichaelBiehn

Life of Pie (2012)
PG/2h 7min/Adventure, Drama, Fantasy/Rate: 7.9/10

A young man who survives a disaster at sea is hurtled into an epic journey of adventure and discovery. While cast away, he forms an unexpected connection with another survivor: a fearsome Bengal tiger.
Director: Ang Lee
Writers: Yann Martel (novel), David Magee (screenplay)
Stars: Suraj Sharma, Irrfan Khan, Adil Hussain

Cast Away (2000)
PG-13/2h 10min/Adventure, Drama, Romance/Rate: 7.8/10

A FedEx executive must transform himself physically and emotionally to survive a crash landing on a deserted island.
Director: Robert Zemeckis
Writer: William Broyles Jr.
Stars: Tom Hanks, Helen Hunt, Paul Sanchez, Lari White

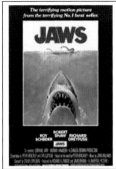

Jaws (1975)
PG/2h 4min/Adventure, Drama, Thriller/Rate: 8.0/10

A local sheriff, a marine biologist and an old seafarer team up to hunt down a great white shark wrecking havoc in a beach resort.
Director: Steven Spielberg
Writers: Peter Benchley and Carl Gottlieb
Stars: Roy Scheider, Robert Shaw, Richard Dreyfuss

Titanic (1997)
PG-13/3h 14min/Drama, Romance/Rate: 7.8/10

A seventeen-year-old aristocrat falls in love with a kind but poor artist aboard the luxurious, ill-fated R.M.S. Titanic.
Director: James Cameron
Writer: James Cameron
Stars: Leonardo DiCaprio, Kate Winslet, Billy Zane

Pirates of the Caribbean: The Curse of the Black Pearl (2003)
PG-13/2h 23min/Action, Adventure, Fantasy/Rate: 8.0/10

Blacksmith Will Turner teams up with eccentric pirate "Captain" Jack Sparrow to save his love, the governor's daughter, from Jack's former pirate allies, who are now undead.
Director: Gore Verbinski
Writers: Ted Elliott, Terry Rossio, Stuart Beattie, Jay Wolpert
Stars: Johnny Depp, Geoffrey Rush, Orlando Bloom

The Admiral (2014) Myeong-ryang (original title)
Not rated/2h 6min/Action, History, War/Rate: 7.2/10

At the strait 'Roaring Currents', master strategist Admiral Yi and his 12 battleships oppose enemy's fleet of 330, and win the most incredible victory of history.
Director: Han-min Kim
Writers: Cheol-hong Jeon, Han-min Kim
Stars: Min-sik Choi, Seung-ryong Ruy, Jin-woong Jo

Finding Nemo (2003)
G/1h 40min/Animation, Adventure, Comedy/Rate: 8.1/10

After his son is captured in the Great Barrier Reef and taken to Sydney, a timid clownfish sets out on a journey to bring him home.
Directors: Andrew Stanton, Lee Unkrich
Writers: Andrew Stanton, Bob Peterson, David Reynolds
Stars: Albert Brooks, Ellen DeGeneres, Alexander Gould

Moana (2016)
PG/1h 47min/Animation, Adventure, Comedy/Rate: 7.6/10

In Ancient Polynesia, when a terrible curse incurred by the Demigod Maui reaches Moana's island, she answers the Ocean's call to seek out the Demigod to set things right.
Directors: Ron Clements, John Musker, Don Hall, Chris Williams
Writers: Jared Bush (screenplay)
Stars: Auli'I Cravalho, Dwayne Johnson, Rachel House

Sailing Forward Categorizing the Ocean Cinema

- In a whole-class discussion, think about the following questions while listening to other teams' summary.
  - o Which movie was most frequently mentioned and why?

  - o Which ocean or sea was identified as the most popular cinematic setting?

  - o What were the common images of the oceans described in the movies?

- [Individual Activity] Based on the shared summaries of pair/group discussion, create your original categories for the ocean cinema. For example, you can focus on the characters of the movies and categorize them into Ocean Survivor Movie, Ocean Traveler Movie, and Ocean Hero Move. Then, make a table with the list of movies belong to each category.

Speaking Tackle 1 Structure of a Good Speech

Just as good writings need structure, so does a good speech. By organizing your ideas with a clear structure, you can deliver your message more clearly and achieve communicative goals more easily.

- Most speeches, no matter how short they are, have "**Opening – Body – Closing**". Can you identify what materials each part often consists of?

	Summary of the main points, Provide some further food for thought, Leave positive memories of your speech, Your final thought/emotion
	Introduction of the speaker and the topic, Engaging the audience's interest, A thought-provoking question, An interesting or controversial statement, A relevant quote or a joke
	Formulating a series of points that you would like to raise, Related points with a logical progression, Evidence or a supporting argument that proves your main idea

- Analyze the structure of your team's and other team' speech. Evaluate how well the structure was organized in terms of its opening-body-closing sequence. Take a note which team left the most positive impression to you and why. Write specific examples of language use or expressions if you can recall them.

Dive into Vocabulary

Search or guess the meanings of vocabulary or phrases below before listening. While listening, make a better guess of the meanings of vocabulary or phrases.

- tadpole (n.)
- salamander (n.)
- microbiological specimen
- science nerd
- "Get a life, kid!"
- neural plasticity
- decay on a curve
- crowd in on ~ To gather closely around someone or something
- defining (adj.)
- gross (v.)
- shelve (v.)
- a marketing hook
- footage (n.)
- wreck (n.)
- impulse (n.)
- catalyst (n.)
- "bearing witness"

Dive into Grammar

James: I probably made that movie because I believed I could actually dive to the Titanic. And **if I could have** actually **dived** to the Titanic without making the movie, I probably **would have done** that.

Use **if + had (could have) + past perfect** followed by
would/could/might + have + past perfect to talk about
the past wish that did not come true ("counterfactual conditional").
Compare **would (do)** with **would have (done)**.

e.g. If I **could have** actually **dived** to the Titanic without making the movie, I probably **would be** a diver instead of a filmmaker by now.

Listening Lighthouse

Listen to the interview of a filmmaker James Cameron.
[NPR] Why did a Hollywood film director journey to the bottom of the ocean?
https://www.npr.org/2014/09/12/342136697/why-did-a-hollywood-film-director-journey-to-the-bottom-of-the-ocean
If necessary, see the transcript at :
http://kuow.org/post/why-did-hollywood-film-director-journey-bottom-ocean

Guiding Questions

1. [Pre-listening] Who is James Cameron?

2. How would you describe James Cameron as a kid?

3. According to the reporter, what is the defining part of James Cameron's movie?

4. Which movie of his was the highest-grossing movie? Which one was the second?

5. Why did James Cameron make Titanic before Avatar?

6. What was James Cameron's primary motivation to make Titanic?

7. Why do you think "bearing witness" matters to James Cameron?

Personal Take
• Which quote or which idea inspired you most in the interview? Why?

Language Portfolio Customize Your Learning

Portfolios are a collection of your own work put together in a file, binder, or online blog. In language learning, you can create your own language portfolios as a way to set up your own goals for learning, to assess your own weaknesses and strengths, to motivate your learning, and to see and measure the progress of yourself during the semester. Language portfolios often consist of three parts:

1. The Passport
This shows an objective documentation of your language education. For example, it may contain certificates or qualifications that are internationally recognized. It may also include test scores you have taken at school or a local language center. Any proof of participation in the activities using English language (e.g. volunteer work, training program, a competition) can also be included to demonstrate your passion in language learning.

2. The Language Biography
This part contains a personal history of your language learning experience and self-assessment materials. You can illustrate your language learning experience in any form – it can be a short narrative about progresses and difficulties you've gone through since you started learning English, it can be a visualized milestone of important events that drew you in to English learning.

In the self-assessment, you can use rather objective criteria such as your abilities in listening, reading, speaking, and writing, or personalized and elaborated goals you have in mind (e.g. "to be able to understand English news articles on a marine topic without difficulties", "to be able to write a 4-paragraph essay within 30 minutes"). Indicate your confidence at the beginning at the semester, and reassess them periodically by the end of semester.

Language Portfolio

3. The Dossier

This is a collection of coursework that shows your English level and use. It may include a summary or note from classroom activities, follow-up homework or personal research related to the course subject, voice or video recordings of a project work that you have produced, or your personal diaries about English learning experiences during the semester.

The textbook recommends a variety of activities and topics that you can further explore in news, videos, and other media, so you can deepen your language and topical learning to any directions that intrigue you. Just don't forget to relate your work with the learning goals that you have set.

[Useful References]

Introduction to and Examples of Language Portfolio by British Council:
https://www.teachingenglish.org.uk/article/portfolios-elt

A Guide for Learners by the European Language Portfolio:
http://www.prosper.ro/EuroIntegrELP/materiale%20pentru%20site%20E
uroIntegrELP_12%20sept/Materials/for%20students/EN_ELP%20Guide
%20for%20learners.pdf

Chapter 2. Marine Weather Forecast

10/02/2016 12:00:00 UTC

Chapter Forecast

- In this chapter, you will learn how to emphasize important points in your speech.
- You will practice how to interpret the marine weather information by understanding technical terms and concepts.
- You will learn practical tips to understand a semi-academic article – by making inference of the meaning of a technical term in a context and following logical flows.

Embark on a Journey   Marine Forecast App

- Form pairs or groups with at least one member in each team having a wifi-connected smartphone. Then, install an open-source app called "**Marine Forecast**" developed by Andreas Fois (available in iTunes or Playstore).
- Open "Weather" menu, enter current GPS location by tapping "GPS", then click "GET WEATHER FORECAST". Discuss:
- o What pieces of information do you see that were not seen in the conventional weather forecast?
- o Why must we be aware of and make use of weather forecast before we head out to the sea? Support your argument with at a concrete example.
- One person in your team will share a brief summary of your findings with the whole class. Remember the tips from **Speaking Tackle 1** (p. 8).

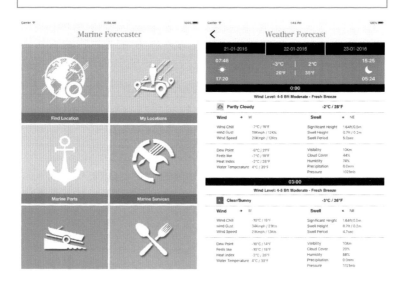

Five Vital Checks when Planning a Boating Trip

The following summary is based on the marine weather checklist developed by the Australian Bureau of Meteorology. Watch the full video at: http://www.bom.gov.au/marine/about/vital-checks.shtml (Turn on captions if necessary.)

1. Pay attention to the warnings.

Warnings are the highest priority forecasts. They warn of potentially dangerous weather conditions expected during the next 24 hours. They cover elements such as wind, weather, sea, and swells. Winds of 26 knots ($\cong 14$ m/s) or more indicate rough conditions for small boats

Type of warning	Average wind speeds indicated
Strong wind	26 to 33 knots
Gale	34 to 47 knots
Storm force	48 to 63 knots
Hurricane	64 knots or more

2. Look at the forecast.

Take note of forecasts indicating reduced visibility from fog or rain, or risks to safety and comfort from thunderstorms, lightning or squall conditions. Some forecasts will also include information on UV levels and the times of day to use sun protection.

3. Take a close look at the wind forecast.

To plan your trip for the best conditions, look for forecast trends in wind speeds and shifts in wind direction over the day. Beware that forecast winds are average wind speeds. Intermittent gusts can reach up to 40% stronger and be even stronger during the storm.

4. Take note of sea and swell conditions.

Forecast waves are average wave heights, and you should be prepared to experience maximum waves of twice the average heights.

Swell waves are the longer, more regular waves generated by distant weather systems. When swell waves reach the shallow water, they start to break and can cause considerable danger near reefs and breakwaters.

Sea waves are generated by local winds, and produce short interval, messy waves, which are often referred to as "choppy conditions".

5. Know when high and low tides are.

Knowing when high and low tide will occur is important for boats entering and exiting river entrances and crossing bars. The combination of an outgoing tidal flow or low tide can cause waves to become steeper than usual, making your boat difficult to navigate.

[Selected Websites for Marine Weather Forecast]
- **Korea Meteorological Administration** (English service is not currently provided.): http://www.weather.go.kr/weather/forecast/marine_daily.jsp
- **Japanese Meteorological Agency:** http://www.jma.go.jp/en/seafcst/
- **National Oceanic and Atmospheric Administration (U.S.):** http://www.nws.noaa.gov/om/marine/home.htm
- **Australian Bureau of Meteorology:** http://www.bom.gov.au/marine

More Elements of Marine Forecast	
	**GPS Coordinates** GPS coordinates are the best way to indicate any location on the globe. GPS coordinates consist of two numbers each representing latitude (North-South location) and longitude (East-West location). The 0 degree line for latitude is called the equator and the 0 degree line for longitude (that passes through Greenwich, London) is called the meridian. The lines of latitude runs parallel and each degree represents the same distance ($\cong$ 111km), whereas the lines of longitude converge at the poles and each degree represents different distances depending on the latitude. Once familiarized, you can make a good guess of GPS coordinates without looking at a map. * How Do GPS Coordinates Work? https://youtu.be/ALN7gXF1thY
	**Wind Direction and Sailing** A wind direction means the direction where the wind is blowing from, not where it's blowing to. For example, a northerly wind (N) blows from the north to the south. A NW wind is a wind that would carry a balloon toward the southeast. When you are sailing, you will always need to know where the wind is coming from. You cannot sail towards about a 120-degree zone to the wind direction.

Unit Conversion for Weather

Weather units are not uniform around the world. So when you are looking at the forecast, pay attention to the units not only the numbers. Most of the weather sites and apps allow you to change the units at the settings.

Wind Speed: 1 MPH = 1.61 km/h = 0.87 kts = 0.45 m/s(MPH: miles per hour, kts: knots)

Temperature: Convert C to F – multiply C by 1.8 and add 32C

Convert F to C – subtract 32 and divide by 1.8

Precipitation: 1 in = 2.54 cm = 25.4 mm (in: inch)

Atmospheric Pressure: 1 in = 33. 864 mb = 33.864 hPa (mb: millibars, hPa: hector Pascals)

Up-to-date Forecast while Sailing

Since the weather conditions can change during the day, it is important for the skipper or master of the vessel to stay tuned to the latest forecast. Marine VHF radio is the best way to access the local weather forecast. VHF radio is transmitted at the high frequency range between 156 and 174 MHz, which is called the VHF maritime mobile band. A marine VHF set also allows you to receive and transmit international callings and distress channel.

Sailing Forward **Navigate Your Ways**

- Now, going back in small teams, each person in the team will choose one coastal area (except for your current location) that one would like to sail tomorrow.

  o Follow the five vital checks using the information on the Marine Forecast app or other websites.

  o Give a weather briefing to each other. Based on the forecast, how do you predict the sailing to be (smooth/tumbling/dangerous)? Is there any time frame that is safer to travel? Try to use 2 or 3 emphasis words from **Speaking Tackle 2** (p. 20).

- [Individual Activity] Based on your conversation, come up with your own sailing plan for tomorrow. Lay out a timetable and plans for activities you would like to do while sailing. Make a note about your clothing and equipment suitable for the weather conditions.

Speaking Tackle 2 Emphasizing Ideas

Once in a while, we experience miscommunication not because we delivered a wrong message, but because we failed to emphasize an important point. Highlighting key ideas in your speech is important to avoid such miscommunication whey you are delivering high priority information, cautions, major decisions, or appealing strong emotions. Observe how people use a variety of structures and expressions to emphasize their messages and enrich your repertoires.

- While watching the "Five Vital Checks" video, take notes what phrases the speaker used to boost the key ideas.

- Try to put a variety of emphasis words in the following sample sentences.
  1) Checking the weather before you sail is (   ).
  2) Fog can have (   ) your visibility.
  3) The wave forecast (   ) when the storm is coming.

Examples of emphasis words
[adjectives] especially important important to note most noteworthy especially relevant fundamental essential vital necessary most valuable
[verbs] should be noted pay particular attention to remember that come first must be considered do not forget
[nouns] a significant factor a primary concern a major event a chief outcome a principal item a key feature a vital force a central issue a substantial point
[others] most of all above all first and foremost most importantly most notably of a high priority of the highest priority one of the most adj. ~s

Dive into Vocabulary

Search or guess the meanings of vocabulary or phrases below before reading. While reading, make a better guess of the meanings of vocabulary or phrases.

- fatality (n.)
- capsize (v.)
- trade wind
- gyre (n.)
- Gulf Stream
- outrun (v.)
- rogue wave
- list (v.)
- on-board accident vs. overboard accident
- run aground
- stationary (adj.)
- buoy (n.)
- moor (v.)
- tether (v.)
- err (v.)

Dive into Grammar

Weather can be difficult to predict, especially on waterways, but good forecasting can **help** ships and their crews **navigate** and **make** decisions that reduce risks.

As shown above, use help and an infinitive with or without **to**:
Jack is helping me **to tidy** my CDs. / Jack is helping me **tidy** my CDs.
I am writing to thank you for helping us **find** the right hotel for our holiday. / I am writing to thank you for helping us **to find** the right hotel for our holiday.
I am trying to help him **look for** a new bike.

Reading Compass

Read the following article on the marine weather forecasting.
https://www.maritimeinjurycenter.com/accidents-and-injuries/weather-forecasting/

Guiding Questions

1. How do winds, waves, swells, and storms influence each other?

2. How is the on-board accident different from the overboard accident?

3. What are the methods used to monitor the weather? What is the relationship between weather monitoring and forecasting?

4. Why does the World Meteorological Organization provide international guidelines for weather forecasting?

5. According to the article, what lesson can we learn from the El Faro accident?

Extended Reading

• Learn more about how meteorologists forecast hurricanes accurately nowadays. What Goes Into Hurricane Forecasting? Satellites, Supercomputers, and More:
https://www.npr.org/sections/thetwo-way/2017/09/08/549477502/what-goes-into-hurricane-forecasting-satellites-supercomputers-and-more

Chapter 3. Marine Tourism

Chapter Forecast

- In this chapter, you will think about how to organize your speech into an effective opening, followed by a body, and a closing.
- You will practice how to share your opinion in a pair or small group, as well as in a whole class setting.
- You will learn practical tips to understand a short interview in a radio – by catching the key words and identifying a main sentence.

Embark on a Journey Your Favorite Oceanfront Cities

- In pairs or groups, talk about the oceanfront cities that you have visited or you would like to visit in the future. Discuss:
  o What are your priorities in choosing a touristic place?
  o What marine activities can you enjoy in the cities?
- Pick two oceanfront cities that your team finds most interesting. One person in a team will deliver a brief presentation about why your team found the cities appealing. Introduce characteristics of each city and some popular touristic spots. Make use of the tips from **Speaking Tackles 1** (p. 8) and 2 (p. 20).

10 Most Beautiful Oceanfront Cities by National Geographic (2014)

Each oceanfront city has its unique charms. Here is the list of ten most beautiful cities selected by National Geographic, which illustrates some examples of beauty and fun you can enjoy at the seaside cities. For the original list and descriptions:
https://www.nationalgeographic.com/travel/photos-top-10-oceanfront-cities/

Tel Aviv, Israel

Also known as the financial center and the technological hub of Israel, Tel Aviv invites you to modern and natural beauty of Mediterranean coastline. The emerald beach has plenty of room for beach bathing. The historic port of Jaffa is also a must-stop, where you can enjoy both art and cuisine at a vibrant gallery, café, and restaurant.

Tallinn, Estonia

The capital of Estonia, Tallinn, presents one of the most intact medieval towns in Europe. It offers a rare experience of wandering around an oceanfront city filled with medieval stone walls, sky-scraping church bell towers, and winding cobblestone streets. You can enjoy the picturesque perch of the Baltic at Lennusadam Seaplane Harbor, with options for cruising, kayaking, and yachting. An interactive maritime museum by the harbor has ships and a submarine to explore.

St. John's, Newfoundland, Canada
Having used as the natural harbor since 1500, St. John is undisputedly the oldest "European" town in North America. With lots of buildings and houses date back as old as Victorian Times, Irish folk music floating from seafront bars is reminiscent of Dublin. The city also struts its unique personality when icebergs float into the harbor and whales spout offshore.

San Diego, California, USA
San Diego has been the economic center of the region by hosting military bases and offering a hub for tourism, trade, and businesses. Its year-around mild climate attracts surfers to the Pacific beaches, while other tourist attractions attract nature and animal lovers such as Balboa Park, San Diego Safari Park, and SeaWorld San Diego. At the south coast, the visitors can tour inside of the 1945 World War II U.S.S.°*Midway*, the country's longest-serving aircraft carrier.

Marseille, France
Founded by Greek traders in 600 B.C., Marseille is a port city where style and history meet. Basilique Notre-Dame de la Garde, which stands on the hilltop of Marseille, has a mesmerizing effect on the visitors. Another architectural beauty is the Museum of European and Mediterranean Civilizations, a square box covered with latticework. From its rooftop, visitors can enjoy the panoramic views of the coastline and parade of yachts heading out to sea.

Perth, Western Australia, Australia

Perth is the capital and the largest city of Western Australia with easy access to sunny and pristine beaches adjacent to Indian Ocean. At the northern coast, visitors can spot sea lions, bottlenose dolphins, and migrating humpback whales along the Marmion Marine Park. If you are a gourmet seeker, Swan Valley is a must stop for food and wine. While walking through King's Park and Botanic Gardens, you can learn about the unique native flora and refresh your minds with diverse sceneries.

Brisbane, Queensland, Australia

As one of the oldest cities in Australia, Brisbane has a face of both worlds: a sophisticated global city and affluent nature in subtropical climate. Visitors can cruise the Brisbane River, explore the South Bank parklands, and take in the panoramic views on the towering Story Bridge climb. Independent stores and designer boutiques along Fortitude Valley sell handmade jewelry, art, antiques, and vintage fashion.

Durban, South Africa

With sunny beaches and Afro-Indian blended cultures, Durban is the continent's busiest seaport. The warm sandy beach of Golden Mile welcomes visitors to its luxury hotels, trendy clubs, and beachside restaurants. At the end of the beach, have some fun at Ushaka Marine World and shop for ethnic clothing and souvenirs at Village Walk. You can also take in a Zulu experience at PheZulu Safari Park and learn about the culture of South Africa's largest ethnic group.

Vladivostok, Primorsky Krai, Russia

Vladivostok is Russia's remote window to the Far East, located around the Golden Horn Bay. Serving as one of Russia's most important commercial ports and naval bases, the city boasts great views along the bay. Most spectacular is the foggy views from Russky Bridge, a cable-stayed bridge connecting Russky Island to the main peninsula.

The city also offers unique pan-Asian cuisines, reflecting its long history of interactions with Korea, China, and Japan.

Portland, Maine, USA

This New England city is rather less populated, but lively place well known for its top-end galleries and waterfront lobster shacks. The most visit worthy site is the postcard-ready Portland Head Light at Cape Elizabeth. You can visit the lighthouse museum and walk up and down the coastal cliffs around the park, tracing the early history of America.

Sailing Forward Plan Your Own Trip

- Now, individually or in group, make a 3-day travel plan of one oceanfront city of your choice. Follow the instructions below:
  o At the top, write a short introduction of the city and reasons to visit the city.
  o Outline the approximate timeline for each day of travel. Decide which places you will visit, for how long, and what you will do in each place.
  o Include at least three activities related to a marine theme.
  o Use relevant maps, photos, and images if you would like.

A Sample travel plan

Our Dream Travel to Okinawa, Japan		
Okinawa is one of the islands of Japan, which used to be an independent nation, Rhyukyu Kingdom until 1879. Okinawans, therefore, are known to celebrate their distinctive ethnic culture and identity from mainstream Japanese. The tropical weather allows people to obtain rich marine resources and to access beautiful natural beaches everywhere in the island. Our group chose Okinawa because we were attracted to both its rich cultural heritage and clean marine environment.		
DAY 1	DAY 2	DAY 3
8am Arriving at Naha Airport	8am Eating breakfast at the local seafood soba restaurant	8am Eating local breakfast with seasonal fish at *Kokusai Douri*
10am Check in at the resort hotel at *Busena* beach area ...	9am-12pm Visiting *Churaumi Aquarium* ...	9-12pm Visiting *Himeyuri Peace Museum* ...

Writing Tackle 1 Writing an Email

Writing an email in English is not only a foundational skill required in many workplaces, but can be a good opportunity to practice English writing. It doesn't have to be too formal. In fact, the very point of email is to write meaningful messages through an instant and less formal medium.

Try to build a habit to get in touch with friends through English emails. Communicating in email with friends you've met via offline or social media will require a particular set of skills, but you will learn to enjoy the experience of extended and embellished communications. For example, in this class, you can choose a partner who also wants to practice English writing through email, and share your travel plans to an oceanfront city. You can practice writing emails with various purposes (e.g. invitation, request, inquiry, complain, making an appointment, etc.) if you would like. You can also give feedback to each other about how clear the email was and recommend each other how one could write better or differently to facilitate understanding and respect other's feelings.

Instead of drowning in spam or unsolicited emails, fill your mailbox with meaningful exchanges. In so doing,

- Reflect on your strengths and weaknesses when communicating with others through emails,
- Observe how others write emails using different repertoires,
- Think about tips to write good emails.

There is no magic recipe to write great emails from the beginning, but for sure, repeated exchanges will make your identity as an English writer stronger while searching for the best recipe that works for you.

Dive into Vocabulary

Search or guess the meanings of vocabulary or phrases below before listening. While listening, make a better guess of the meanings of vocabulary or phrases.

- rugged (adj.)
- a shooting location
- devoted to ~
- snake up
- assassin (n.)
- draw (v.)
- local (n.)
- mirror (v.)
- sectarian (adj.)
- 1998 Good Friday Agreement
- IRA (Irish Republican Army)
- annual revenue
- chronologically (adv.)
- heyday (n.)
- boomtown (n.)
- replica (n.)
- shipyard (n.)
- furnace (n.)
- hull (n.)
- rivet (n.)
- maiden voyage
- stone deaf
- watch out for ~
- the heart of the city
- a Methodist minister
- decommission (v.)

Listening Lighthouse

Listen to the news on the booming tourism in Northern Ireland.
[NPR] After avoiding the country for decades, tourists are now flocking to Northern Ireland
https://www.npr.org/2017/11/14/564163442/after-avoiding-the-country-for-decades-tourists-are-now-flocking-to-northern-ire
If necessary, refer to the transcript on the same page.

Guiding Questions

1. What does Stephen McNally do for living? (What was his job career before the 1998 peace agreement?)

2. Why didn't people come to Belfast for tourism before 1998?

Listening Lighthouse

3. How does Mr. McNally feel about the change in tourism industry?

4. Besides the "Game of Thrones" shooting locations, what attracts people to come to Belfast?

5. What can visitors see and experience in the museum?

6. Why do some people feel safer to visit Belfast than London?

Personal Take

• Which quote or which idea inspired you most in this report? Why?

• Come up with your original idea to revitalize tourism of a waterfront city that you know.

Chapter 4. Oceans and Literature

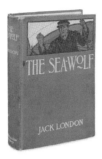 

Chapter Forecast

- In this chapter, you will learn how images, rhymes, and narratives are used in literature genres (poetry and novel) to reveal our emotion and subjectivity.
- You will practice how to express your sentiment and feelings as you read and write literature pieces.
- You will appreciate how masterful writers relate themselves to the world by creating a unique character or persona in their writings.

Embark on a Journey **Sea Poems**

- [HOMEWORK] Find a sea poem that speaks to your heart. The poem can be either in English or in other languages that you speak.
  - o If you have chosen an English poem, highlight images that describe the sea. With a different color, highlight words that reveal feelings.
  - o If you have chosen a poem in other languages, translate it in English.
- [IN-CLASS] Divide into English poem groups and translated poem groups.
  - o In English poem groups, discuss how you relate the images of the sea to the speaker's attitude toward the sea. Share why you liked the poem.
  - o In translated poem groups, share your translations with others. Discuss what you enjoyed and what you found difficult while translating.
  - o In a whole-class discussion, share the summary of pair/group discussions.

MY BOUNTY IS AS BOUNDLESS AS THE SEA,
MY LOVE AS DEEP;
THE MORE I GIVE TO THEE,
THE MORE I HAVE,
FOR BOTH ARE INFINITE.

WILLIAM SHAKESPEARE
ROMEO AND JULIET

바다는 나에게 / 이해인	The Sea is to Me / Hae-in Lee
바다는 가끔 내가 좋아하는 삼촌처럼 곁에 있다	The sea often Stays by my side Like my favorite uncle.
나의 이야길 잘 들어 주다가도 어느 순간 내가 힘들다고 하소연하면 "엄살은 무슨? 복에 겨운 투정이 야" 하고 못 들은 척한다	He listens to me all ears, But in a moment when I Whine about hardship, "Why make a big fuss? You're grumbling about too much luck." He pretends like he didn't hear a thing.
어느 날 내가 갖고 싶은 것들을 하나하나 부탁하면 금방 구해줄 것처럼 다정하게 "그래, 알았어" 하다가도 "너무 욕심이 많군!" 하고 꼭 한 마디 해서 나를 무안하게 한다	One day when I ask for The things I want one by one, As if it will get those soon, it kindly replies, "Ok. Got it." followed by "Too greedy!" Those added words Make me embarrassing.
바다는 나에게 삼촌처럼 정겹고 든든한 푸른 힘이다	The sea is to me, Like my uncle, friendly and faithful Blue power.

바다 / 백석	The Sea / Paik Seok
바닷가에 왔더니 바다와 같이 당신이 생각만 나는구려 바다와 같이 당신을 사랑하고만 싶구려	Having come to the seaside, It only makes me think about you with the sea, It only makes me want to love you with the sea.
구붓하고 모래톱을 오르면 당신이 앞선 것만 같구려 당신이 뒤선 것만 같구려	Crawling up the sand bank, It feels like you are ahead, It feels like you are behind.
그리고 지중지중 물가를 거닐면 당신이 이야기를 하는 것만 같구려 당신이 이야기를 끊는 것만 같구려	Then idly walking the waterside, It feels like you are telling stories, It feels like you are breaking stories.
바닷가는 개지꽃*에 개지 아니 나오고 고기비눌에 하이얀 햇볕만 쇠리쇠리하야 어쩐지 쓸쓸만 하구려 섧기만 하구려	On the seaside, No puppy coming out of puppy flower*, Only white sunlight flashing on the fish scale, It feels lonely and sorrowful.
* 개지꽃: 나팔꽃의 평안도 방언	* Puppy flower: a Northern Korean dialect for morning glory

I started Early – Took my Dog – / Emily Dickenson

I started Early – Took my Dog –
And visited the Sea –
The Mermaids in the Basement
Came out to look at me –

And Frigates – in the Upper Floor
Extended Hempen Hands –
Presuming Me to be a Mouse –
Aground – opon the Sands –

But no Man moved Me – till the Tide
Went past my simple Shoe –
And past my Apron - and my Belt
And past my Boddice – too –

And made as He would eat me up –
As wholly as a Dew
Opon a Dandelion's Sleeve –
And then – I started – too –

And He – He followed – close behind –
I felt His Silver Heel
Opon my Angle – Then my Shoes
Would overflow with Pearl –

Until We met the Solid Town –
No One He seemed to know –
And bowing – with a Mighty look –
At me – The Sea withdrew -

For recitation & resources: https://www.poetryfoundation.org/poems/50976/
i-started-early-took-my-dog-656#tab-resources
For animated recitation: https://youtu.be/kLzmwiyzH1Y

Sea Fever / John Masefield

I must go down to the seas again, to the lonely sea and the sky,
And all I ask is a tall ship and a star to steer her by;
And the wheel's kick and the wind's song and the white sail's shaking,
And a grey mist on the sea's face, and a grey dawn breaking.

I must go down to the seas again, for the call of the running tide
Is a wild call and a clear call that may not be denied;
And all I ask is a windy day with the white clouds flying,
And the flung spray and the blown spume, and the sea-gulls crying.

I must go down to the seas again, to the vagrant gypsy life,
To the gull's way and the whale's way where the wind's like a whetted knife;
And all I ask is a merry yarn from a laughing fellow-rover,
And quiet sleep and a sweet dream when the long trick's over.

For resources:
https://www.poetryfoundation.org/poems/54932/sea-fever-56d235e0d871e
For recitation by the poet himself: https://youtu.be/TCYsLqV2CyU

Sailing Forward **Rhymes in Poetry**

- [Whole Class] Find out rhyming words in English poems.
  - o Find rhyming words in "I started Early –Took my Dog". Where are they located? Does the poem have regular rhymes?
  - o Find rhyming words in "Sea Fever". Where are they located? Does the poem have regular rhymes?
  - o Find rhyming words in the English poem you have searched, and identify what kinds of rhymes it used. (Refer to the table below for the kinds of rhymes.) Share the examples with the classmates.
  - o What do you think are the roles of rhymes in poetry?
  - o When translating poems, how would you account for rhymes?

Kinds of Rhymes	Explanation and examples
Full rhymes	When the ending consonants and vowels of the words match. e.g. tide-ride, wave-cave, ocean-motion…
Semi-rhymes	Match up, but one of the words has an extra syllable. e.g. wait-dating, down-grounded…
Slant rhymes	Match only the ending consonants not the vowels. e.g. salt-insult, seagull-angel…
Forced rhymes	Match up when one of the words stresses an unstressed syllable. e.g. spring-loving, squid-landed…
Visual rhymes	Words that ending syllables look the same but sound different e.g. dove-move, marine-mine…

Writing Tackle 2 Composing Sea Poems

You may thing that writing poetry is reserved for trained poets. However, it can be a good brain teaser for the beginning writers since it requires brainstorming of rich vocabulary while it doesn't require much time to complete a piece.

In this class, each of you are encouraged to express your own feelings toward the sea through poetry and add it to your portfolio. If writing an original poem feels like too much burden, you can start from writing a parody of a poem that you like.

- Make a list of words related to the sea that appear in your mind. Contemplate what feelings and memories those words awaken.
- Write a list of good rhyming words for the list of words you have written. Refer to rhyming dictionaries available online if you need help.
- If you are composing an original poem, write the first full line of poetry. Then, write line by line like you are moving on to the next scene. Look for connections between words and images to spark the poem. Revise your poem to match a rhyme scheme.
- If you are writing a parody, choose the key words or images in the poem that you would like to replace. Find words that you like to replace them with from your list of words. Then, alter the other parts to express your feelings and match a rhyme scheme.

You can also share your poems with the class through an in-class sea poem exhibit or a poem recitation contest. Just remember, being upfront with your feelings and confronting fear is a step that everyone takes to become a fluent language user.

Dive into Vocabulary

The following marine lives appear in the novel The Old Man and The Sea. Think about what Santiago (the old man) knows about the animals as they appear in the novel.

- agua mala: (Spanish) jellyfish; Portuguese man-of-war.
- albacore: a tuna with unusually long pectoral fins, important as a game and food fish in all warm seas.
- barracuda: any of a family of fierce, pikelike tropical fish: some species are edible.
- big blue runner: any of various edible jack fishes of warm seas, as a bluish species and a striped bluish species.
- dolphin: a game fish with colors that brighten and change when the fish is taken out of the water
- dorado: (Spanish) gilding or gilt (literally); here a descriptive term for the golden dolphin
- flying fish: a warm-sea fish with winglike pectoral fins that enable it to glide through the air
- green turtle, hawk-bill, loggerhead: turtles
- mako: a mackerel shark (dentuso in Spanish) that is a voracious and frightening killer known for its rows of large, sharp teeth
- man-of-war bird: a frigate bird which is a seabird found across tropical and subtropical oceans. It has predominantly black plumage with a long forked tail.
- marlin: any of several large, slender, deep-sea billfishes
- plankton: the usually microscopic animal and plant life found floating or drifting in the ocean or in bodies of fresh water, used as food by nearly all aquatic animals
- Sargasso weed:
- sardine: a common name used to refer to various small, oily fish in the herring family.
- shovel-nosed sharks: the scavenger sharks (galanos in Spanish) that destroy the marlin.
- tiburon: (Spanish) shark
- yellow jack: an edible, gold-and-silver marine jack fish found near Florida and the West Indies.

But he crowded the current a little so that he was still fishing correctly though faster than he **would have fished** if he was not trying to use the bird.

We can use **if + had (could have) + past perfect** followed by **would/could/might + have + past perfect** to talk about the past wish that did not come true ("counterfactual conditional"). Compare **would (do)** with **would have (done)**.

Reading Compass

Read the following excerpt from the novel The Old Man and The Sea while answering the questions. The selected pages are from the day two of the novel, when Santiago, the old man, sets out to the sea after the eighty-fourth consecutive days without catching a fish. You are encouraged to read the entire novel if you wish to (copyrights-free copies available on the web).

For the summary and analysis of the entire novel, refer to the following links.
• Sparksnotes summary and analysis: http://www.sparknotes.com/lit/ oldman//
• The Old Man and The Sea (short animated film): https://youtu.be/W5ih1IRIRxI

Guiding Questions

1. [32] What does Santiago notice as he saw a man-of-war bird?

2. [32-33] What does he speculate when he saw a school of flying fish?

3. [33] Why didn't he chase the school of flying fish and dolphin?

4. [34-35] Why did he swear at aqua mala or Portuguese men-of-war?

5. [36] Why does Santiago consume turtle eggs? How does he feel about turtles

Reading Compass

6. [37-38] What for did Santiago catch a tuna or albacore?

7. [38] Why is the old man not bothered by the fact that he is talking to himself?

8. [39] What does Santiago think that he is born for?

9. [40] What kind of fish did he expect it to be when he felt tension in his line?

10. [43-44] Why nothing has happened when Santiago pulled the line?

Personal Take

• How would you describe Santiago's character and personality? What do you think are his virtues as a seaman?

• Why do you think Santiago pursuits a big fish instead of a school of small fish? Can you relate the reasons with his character and personality?

• How are the marine lives in this novel described? How would you describe Santiago's attitude towards the marine lives and the sea?

From *The Old Man and the Sea*, Earnest Hemmingway (1952), pp. 32-44

[Number] indicate the page of the original copy of the novel.

Just then he saw a man-of-war bird with his long black wings circling in the sky ahead of him. He made a quick drop, slanting down on his back-swept wings, and then circled again.

"He's got something," the old man said aloud. "He's not just looking."

He rowed slowly and steadily toward where the bird was circling. He did not hurry and he kept his lines straight up and down. But he crowded the current a little so that he was still fishing correctly though faster than he would have fished if he was not trying to use the bird.

The bird went higher in the air and circled again, his wings motionless. Then he dove suddenly and the old man saw flying fish spurt out of the water and sail desperately over the surface.

[33] "Dolphin," the old man said aloud. "Big dolphin."

He shipped his oars and brought a small line from under the bow. It had a wire leader and a medium-sized hook and he baited it with one of the sardines. He let it go over the side and then made it fast to a ring bolt in the stern. Then he baited another line and left it coiled in the shade of the bow. He went back to rowing and to watching the long-winged black bird who was working, now, low over the water.

As he watched the bird dipped again slanting his wings for the dive and then swinging them wildly and ineffectually as he followed the flying fish. The old man could see the slight bulge in the water that the big dolphin raised as they followed the escaping fish. The dolphin were cutting through the water below the flight of the fish and would be in the water, driving at speed, when the fish dropped. It is a big school of dolphin, he thought. They are widespread and the flying fish have little chance. The bird has no chance. The flying fish are too big for him and they go too fast.

He watched the flying fish burst out again and again and the ineffectual movements of the bird. That school has gotten away from me, he thought. They are moving out too fast and too far. But perhaps I will pick up [34] a stray and perhaps my big fish is around them. My big fish must be somewhere.

The clouds over the land now rose like mountains and the coast was only a long green line with the gray blue hills behind it. The water was a dark blue now, so dark that it was almost purple. As he looked down into it he saw the red sifting of the plankton in the dark water and the strange light the sun made now. He watched his lines to see them go straight down out of sight into the water and he was happy to see so much plankton because it meant fish. The strange light the sun made in the water, now that the sun was higher, meant good weather and so did the shape of the clouds over the land. But the bird was almost out of sight now and nothing showed on the surface of the water but some patches of yellow, sun-bleached Sargasso weed and the purple, formalized, iridescent, gelatinous bladder of a Portuguese man-of-war floating dose beside the boat. It turned on its side and then righted itself. It floated cheerfully as a bubble with its long deadly purple filaments trailing a yard behind it in the water.

"Agua mala," the man said. "You whore."

From where he swung lightly against his oars he looked down into the water and saw the tiny fish that [35] were coloured like the trailing filaments and swam between them and under the small shade the bubble made as it drifted. They were immune to its poison. But men were not and when same of the filaments would catch on a line and rest there slimy and purple while the old man was working a fish, he would have welts and sores on his arms and hands of the sort that poison ivy or poison oak can give. But these poisonings from the agua mala came quickly and struck like a whiplash.

The iridescent bubbles were beautiful. But they were the falsest thing in the sea and the old man loved to see the big sea turtles eating them. The turtles saw them, approached them from the front, then shut their eyes so they were completely carapaced and ate them filaments and all. The old man loved to see the turtles eat them and he loved to walk on them on the beach after a storm and hear them pop when he stepped on them with the horny soles of his feet.

He loved green turtles and hawk-bills with their elegance and speed and their great value and he had a friendly contempt for the huge, stupid loggerheads, yellow in their armour-plating, strange in their [36] love-making, and happily eating the Portuguese men-of-war with their eyes shut.

He had no mysticism about turtles although he had gone in turtle boats for many years. He was sorry for them all, even the great trunk backs that were as long as the skiff and weighed a ton. Most people are heartless about turtles because a turtle's heart will beat for hours after he has been cut up and butchered. But the old man thought, I have such a heart too and my feet and hands are like theirs. He ate the white eggs to give himself strength. He ate them all through May to be strong in September and October for the truly big fish.

He also drank a cup of shark liver oil each day from the big drum in the shack where many of the fishermen kept their gear. It was there for all fishermen who wanted it. Most fishermen hated the taste. But it was no worse than getting up at the hours that they rose and it was very good against all colds and grippes and it was good for the eyes.

Now the old man looked up and saw that the bird was circling again.

"He's found fish," he said aloud. No flying fish broke the surface and there was no scattering of bait [37] fish. But as the old man watched, a small tuna rose in the air, turned and dropped head first into the water. The tuna shone silver in the sun and after he had dropped back into the water another and another rose and they were jumping in all directions, churning the water and leaping in long jumps after the bait. They were circling it and driving it.

If they don't travel too fast I will get into them, the old man thought, and he watched the school working the water white and the bird now dropping and dipping into the bait fish that were forced to the surface in their panic.

"The bird is a great help," the old man said. Just then the stern line came taut under his foot, where he had kept a loop of the line, and he dropped his oars and felt tile weight of the small tuna's shivering pull as he held the line firm and commenced to haul it in. The shivering increased as he pulled in and he could see the blue back of the fish in the water and the gold of his sides before he swung him over the side and into the boat. He lay in the stern in the sun, compact and bullet shaped, his big, unintelligent eyes staring as he thumped his life out against the planking of the boat with the quick shivering strokes of his neat, fast-moving [38] tail. The old man hit him on the head

for kindness and kicked him, his body still shuddering, under the shade of the stern.

"Albacore," he said aloud. "He'll make a beautiful bait. He'll weigh ten pounds."

He did not remember when he had first started to talk aloud when he was by himself. He had sung when he was by himself in the old days and he had sung at night sometimes when he was alone steering on his watch in the smacks or in the turtle boats. He had probably started to talk aloud, when alone, when the boy had left. But he did not remember. When he and the boy fished together they usually spoke only when it was necessary. They talked at night or when they were storm-bound by bad weather. It was considered a virtue not to talk unnecessarily at sea and the old man had always considered it so and respected it. But now he said his thoughts aloud many times since there was no one that they could annoy.

"If the others heard me talking out loud they would think that I am crazy," he said aloud. "But since I am not crazy, I do not care. And the rich have radios to talk to them in their boats and to bring them the baseball."

[39] Now is no time to think of baseball, he thought. Now is the time to think of only one thing. That which I was born for. There might be a big one around that school, he thought. I picked up only a straggler from the albacore that were feeding. But they are working far out and fast. Everything that shows on the surface today travels very fast and to the north-east. Can that be the time

of day? Or is it some sign of weather that I do not know?

He could not see the green of the shore now but only the tops of the blue hills that showed white as though they were snow-capped and the clouds that looked like high snow mountains above them. The sea was very dark and the light made prisms in the water. The myriad flecks of the plankton were annulled now by the high sun and it was only the great deep prisms in the blue water that the old man saw now with his lines going straight down into the water that was a mile deep.

The tuna, the fishermen called all the fish of that species tuna and only distinguished among them by their proper names when they came to sell them or to trade them for baits, were down again. The sun was [40] hot now and the old man felt it on the back of his neck and felt the sweat trickle down his back as he rowed.

I could just drift, he thought, and sleep and put a bight of line around my toe to wake me. But today is eighty-five days and I should fish the day well.

Just then, watching his lines, he saw one of the projecting green sticks dip sharply.

"Yes," he said. "Yes," and shipped his oars without bumping the boat. He reached out for the line and held it softly between the thumb and forefinger of his right hand. He felt no strain nor weight and he held the line lightly. Then it came again. This time it was a tentative pull, not solid nor heavy, and he knew exactly what it was. One hundred fathoms down a marlin was eating the sardines that covered the point and the shank of the hook where the hand-forged hook projected from the head of the small tuna.

The old man held the line delicately, and softly, with his left hand, unleashed it from the stick. Now he could let it run through his fingers without the fish feeling any tension.

This far out, he must be huge in this month, he thought. Eat them, fish. Eat them. Please eat them.

[41] How fresh they are and you down there six hundred feet in that cold water in the dark. Make another turn in the dark and come back and eat them.

He felt the light delicate pulling and then a harder pull when a sardine's head must have been more difficult to break from the hook. Then there was nothing.

"Come on," the old man said aloud. "Make another turn. Just smell them. Aren't they lovely? Eat them good now and then there is the tuna. Hard and cold and lovely. Don't be shy, fish. Eat them."

He waited with the line between his thumb and his finger, watching it and the other lines at the same time for the fish might have swum up or down. Then came the same delicate pulling touch again.

"He'll take it," the old man said aloud. "God help him to take it."

He did not take it though. He was gone and the old man felt

nothing.

"He can't have gone," he said. "Christ knows he can't have gone. He's making a turn. Maybe he has been hooked before and he remembers something of it.

[42] Then he felt the gentle touch on the line and he was happy.

"It was only his turn," he said. "He'll take it."

He was happy feeling the gentle pulling and then he felt something hard and unbelievably heavy. It was the weight of the fish and he let the line slip down, down, down, unrolling off the first of the two reserve coils. As it went down, slipping lightly through the old man's fingers, he still could feel the great weight, though the pressure of his thumb and finger were almost imperceptible.

"What a fish," he said. "He has it sideways in his mouth now and he is moving off with it."

Then he will turn and swallow it, he thought. He did not say that because he knew that if you said a good thing it might not happen. He knew what a huge fish this was and he thought of him moving away in the darkness with the tuna held crosswise in his mouth. At that moment he felt him stop moving but the weight was still there. Then the weight increased and he gave more line. He tightened the pressure of his thumb and finger for a moment and the weight increased and was going straight down.

[43] "He's taken it," he said. "Now I'll let him eat it well."

He let the line slip through his fingers while he reached down with his left hand and made fast the free end of the two reserve coils to the loop of the two reserve coils of the next line. Now he was ready. He had three forty-fathom coils of line in reserve now, as well as the coil he was using.

"Eat it a little more," he said. "Eat it well."

Eat it so that the point of the hook goes into your heart and kills you, he thought. Come up easy and let me put the harpoon into you. All right. Are you ready? Have you been long enough at table?

"Now!" he said aloud and struck hard with both hands, gained a yard of line and then struck again and again, swinging with each arm alternately on the cord with all the strength of his arms and the pivoted weight of his body.

Nothing happened. The fish just moved away slowly and the old man could not raise him an inch. His line was strong and made for heavy fish and he held it against his hack until it was so taut that beads of water were jumping from it. Then it began to make a slow hissing sound in the water and he still held it, bracing [44] himself against the thwart and leaning back against the pull. The boat began to move slowly off toward the north-west.

Chapter 5. The World of Marine Bio-Resources

Chapter Forecast

- In this chapter, you will learn how to verbally describe visual data, and convert verbal information through visuals.
- You will practice how to deliver a mini presentation using charts and graphs in front of small audience under time pressure.
- You will observe and learn how visuals can be used in news and academic articles to support the main idea.

Embark on a Journey Types of Charts and Graphs

- [Homework] Individually, search and save/print three different charts or graphs related to marine bio-resources.

- In pairs or groups,

    o Group them together based on the types of charts or graphs.

    o Identify the names of the type of charts or graphs if you can.

    o Discuss what kinds of the data each type of charts or graphs deals with. (e.g. qualitative data vs. quantitative data, category vs. number, proportion vs. amount)

- As a whole class, synthesize your findings through a teacher-led discussion.

    o What type of charts or graphs seems to be most frequently used?

    o What kind of themes the charts and graphs frequently describe?

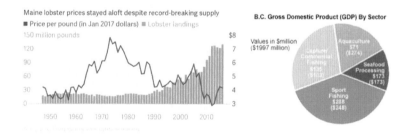

Types of Charts and Graphs	
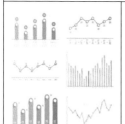	**Bar / Line Charts** - **Purpose**: To make comparisons of data on two or more variables (often expressed in x-axis and *y-axis*), to show a relationship or pattern of two or more variables - Bar charts are more suitable to express relationships between categories and quantities (e.g. gender and heights), whereas line charts are more suitable to express relationships between quantities (e.g. age and heights).
Elements 	**Venn Diagrams** - **Purpose**: To show logical relations between a collection of different sets - Let's say there are two sets: A and B. The combined region of A and B is called the *union* of A and B (A ∪ B). The overlapped region of A and B is called *intersection* of A and B (°A ∩ B).
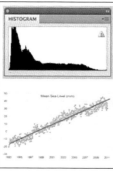	**Histograms / Scatter Plots** - **Purpose**: To visualize the distribution of the data on two or more variables (often expressed in *x-axis* and *y-axis*) - While bar or line charts show data through a representative value (i.e. average), histograms or scatter plots indicate all the values on a graph, showing frequencies as well as quantities.

	**Word Clouds** - **Purpose**: To visualize the frequency distribution of words with textual data - This is a rather new form representing word distribution, but has become quite popular these days. If you search 'word cloud generator' on the web, there are a number of online software that allows you to make your original word clouds.
	**Candlestick Chart** - **Purpose**: To show trends while also indicating value movements in shorter intervals, most frequently showing stock price trends over time - For each candlestick, the square part is called 'real body', showing the opening and closing value. The upper line is called 'upper shadow' and the lower line 'lower shadow', indicating highest and lowest value movements.
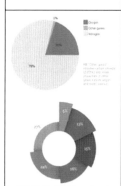	**Pie / Doughnut Charts** - **Purpose**: To illustrate composition expressed in numerical proportion - Each segment is called 'slice', just like a pizza. When explaining the charts, describe proportions in various ways such as '1/3' (one thirds), a quarter, percentage, and decimal point.
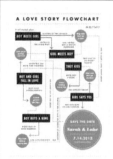	**Flow / Process Charts** - **Purpose**: To show the logical flow or process, often used to guide a decision - Each flowchart has its own repertoire of boxes and notational conventions, but most commonly a rectangular box is used to denote a processing step, and a diamond box to denote a decision step.

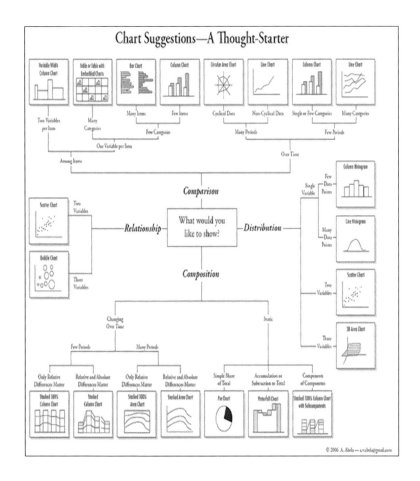

Chart Suggestions—A Thought-Starter

Sailing Forward **Presentation Karaoke**

• Now, going back in small teams, play the game called 'Presentation Karaoke' with the marine bio-resources charts you have prepared. Follow the rules below. Refer to **Speaking Tackle 3** on the next page.

o *Player A* in a team will choose and show three marine bio-resources charts in a random order, and *Player B* will have to explain the data appearing on a chart as if he/she knows the charts well.

o *Player B* will have 10-15 seconds to look at the chart and prepare, 30-45 seconds to explain the data. Be flexible in time if necessary. Explain:

(a) What the chart show (e.g. "The pie chart here shows ~.")

(b) The general trend of the chart (e.g. "In general, the catch of salmon gradually decreased from 1970s to 2000.")

(c) One or two points that need to be noted (e.g. "There was a sudden drop in seafood production in the year 2011 due to an oil spill accident.")

(d) Conclusion or interpretation (e.g. "I think it is necessary to regulate the catch of salmon to protect marine industry in a long-term.")

o *Player A* will measure time and take a note whether or not Player B has explained the data correctly. Give feedback at the end of three consecutive presentations.

o Take turns and repeat the game.

Speaking Tackle 3 Explaining Data

If you use a variety of expressions to describe data, you can make people understand the visuals more easily and accurately. Read the following descriptions of imaginary data, and imagine how the charts or graphs look like.

Comparison /Relationships	- **The x-axis shows** time by the year, **the y-axis shows** the prices of seafood in dollars. - The price of salmon **was highest / reached the peak** in the year 1995. **(lowest / hit the bottom)** During 1990s, the price of salmon **was higher than** the price of shrimp in Canada.
Distribution	- In general, there is **a positive correlation between** temperature and the appearance of algae. **(a negative correlation)** - Especially when the sea temperature **is ranged between** 23-25°C, algae **is observed most frequently.**
Trends	- As you can see, **the overall trend is downward. (upward)** - If you see the red line, the total fish catch of Norway **was the highest among the three countries** from 1988 to 1993, but it **ranked second** from 1994 to 1999. It **hit the bottom** in 2000, but it **showed a sharp increase** from 2001 to 2005. - The amount of fish caught in Denmark **changed most dramatically.** It **ranked top** until 1994, but **remained steady afterwards.** Other countries **caught up** its amount of fish catch, and from 2001 to 2005, it even **ranked last** among three countries.
Composition	- **Three most popular sushi fish groups are** tuna, salmon, and eel, and they **account for more than 80 percent** of total sushi fish. - Tuna **make up the largest group** among fish consumed for sushi, which **comprises over a third** of all the sushi fish. - Salmon and eel **make up the second and third largest**, and they **represent about a quarter** of the sushi fish respectively.

Dive into Vocabulary

Search or guess the meanings of vocabulary or phrases below before reading. While reading, make a better guess of the meanings of vocabulary or phrases.

- dwindle (v.)
- take steps
- sevenfold increase
- in dire need of ~
- sliding catch limit
- resilient (adj.)
- replenish (v.)
- come on the heels of ~
- bar (n.)
- hand-wringing (n.)
- preliminary (adj.)
- robustly (adv.)

Dive into Grammar

There is concern that what appears to be population growth in the Western Atlantic bluefin **could be** inflated because Eastern bluefin have been migrating over and mixing with the Western stock.

We can use **if + had (could have) + past perfect** followed by **would/could/might + have + past perfect** to talk about the past wish that did not come true ("counterfactual conditional"). Compare **would (do)** with **would have (done)**.

e.g. If I could have actually dived to the Titanic without making the movie, I probably **would be** a diver instead of a filmmaker by now.

Reading Compass

Read the following news on the recent agreement of Pacific bluefin tuna recovery.

[NPR] Countries Pledge to Recover Dwindling Pacific Bluefin Tuna Population:
https://www.npr.org/sections/thesalt/2017/09/01/547903557/countries-ple
dge-to-recover-dwindling-pacific-bluefin-tuna-population

Guiding Questions

1. What happened in a joint meeting in Busan on Friday? (who, what, how, why?)

2. How big are the current stocks of Pacific bluefin compared to their historic size?

3. Other than the 20 percent target to rebuild the Pacific bluefin population by 2034, what detailed agreement has been made?

4. What announcement has been made in the U.S. right before the agreement? (who, what, how, why?)

5. Why Pacific bluefin tuna was not listed as an endangered species in by the U.S. federal government?

6. Why scientists are cautious to view that the Atlantic bluefin tuna population has fully recovered?

Visualize Reading

- Based on this article, draft a chart that shows the historical, current and projected Pacific bluefin tuna population.

- Now, search on the web an actual chart that shows the Pacific bluefin tuna population. If you cannot find one, follow the link below and refer to Figure1.
  http://apjjf.org/2016/15/Gilhooly.html

  o How much were the historical and current levels of the Pacific bluefin tuna population?

  o How would you describe the general trend to be?

  o What other patterns did you find interesting in the chart?

Personal Take

- Do you agree or disagree to the following statement? "Commercial fishing needs to be controlled and managed by international agreements."

Chapter 6. Energy from the Ocean

Chapter Forecast

- In this chapter, you will learn how to take turns in a discussion both to reveal your position clearly and to be polite.

- You will practice how to acknowledge pros and cons regarding a topic, and use them in a discussion to develop your opinion.

- You will practice how to understand a news report dealing with contested positions on an issue.

Embark on a Journey **Marine-based Energy**

- In pairs or groups, come up with sources of energy that are coming from the oceans.   Make a list and discuss for each source of energy:

  o Whether or not it is a renewable source.

  o Whether or not it causes damage to the oceans. If it does, what damage?

  o Whether or not it is applicable in your country/region of residence.

  o Whether or not you will support the installation of the facilities for the energy source in your place of residence. What are the reasons?

- After the pair or small-group discussion, choose one marine-based energy source that you are most eager to support its development. Write a bullet-listed pros and cons memo for your favorite marine-based energy source.

Pros and Cons in Marine-based Energy

The term *marine energy* generally refers to the energy generated by waves, tides, salinity, and ocean temperature differences. Since the movement of oceanic water creates a large sum of kinetic energy, it can be harnessed to generate electricity. Offshore wind power is typically not considered as marine energy because it's driven by the wind. Offshore petroleum and natural gas, which account for about 30% of crude oil and natural gas production, are also not called marine energy because they are simply fossil fuels. Therefore, we will use the term *marine-based energy* as an umbrella term to cover all these energy sources.

The following table explains the mechanisms of marine-based energy and enlists some of the pros and cons. However, all the points listed here can be disputed with detailed counter-arguments.

 **1. Offshore Oil and Natural Gas**	**Mechanism** They can be obtained from offshore oil drilling which takes place under ocean water, typically ranging from 400 to 1,500 meters. Ultra-deepwater drilling may reach up to 3,000 meters with technological advancement. Just like onshore oil and gas, the initial well is drilled and pipes are installed to extract oil and gas. Offshore shale gas, a layer of gas stored under impermeable rock (shale rock), is also becoming a popular target for extraction.
Pros • Offshore wells tend to produce more oil/gas per day and have a longer lifespan than onshore wells. • Oil and gas are two of the major sources (more than 50%) of the world's energy consumption. • Oil and gas have more technological options to store and transport than other energy sources. • Due to the prior reason, they are easier to export to other regions and countries.	**Cons** • Reservoirs are limited and will be depleted. • Due to the increased difficulty of drilling in deep water, it tends to cost more than onshore drilling. • Profitability fluctuates due to market factors. • Oil spill can cause water pollution, and combustion air pollution. • Increased use of fossil fuels is thought to be the biggest cause of global warming.

	Mechanism
 **2. Offshore Wind Power**	Wind power is the fastest growing alternative to fossil fuels. Since offshore wind is more constant in terms of speed and direction, the efficiency of turbines increases. Turbines can be either installed on the seabed or can "float" on the ocean with the latest technology. Offshore wind power is especially popular in Europe, with Denmark and Germany leading the industry.
Pros • Relies on clean and renewable energy source (the wind) and doesn't consume water. • More effective (larger scale + higher wind speed + no physical obstructions) and less intrusive than onshore windmills. • Operational cost is low and stable. • It's fastest growing renewable energy.	**Cons** • May affect local fishing and aquafarming. • May ruin the ocean view. • May increase the chance of marine accidents for workers and vessels. • Initial installation and energy transmission can cost a lot. With the current technology, the generators cost 90% more than fossil fuels, 50% more than nuclear.
 **3. Tide and Wave Power**	**Mechanism** The kinetic energy of tide and wave is harnessed through various devices such as one using the rush of air tapped by waves/tides to rotate blades and spin an electric generator. Experimental plants are running in many countries, but few of the plants are producing power at a competitive price.
Pros • Relies on clean and renewable energy source (hydropower). • Tidal power draws energy from the Moon's gravitational force, which is one of the most predictable powers (not affected by weather or other conditions). • Can avoid concerns over impact on the natural landscape.	**Cons** • Few commercial scale generators are available. (One of them is in South Korea, Sihwa Lake Tidal Power Station.) • Most installation needs to be large-scale to make it economical. (Mostly done at a national level than by private companies) • It is likely to have more impact on marine life due to underwater setups.

4. Ocean Thermal Energy

Mechanism

Thermo energy is converted into kinetic energy to spin a generator. It uses the temperature difference between surface and deep water. Warm surface seawater is pumped into the plant, passes through heat exchanger, and boils liquid ammonia (which has a very low boiling point) into a pressurized vapor. This gas will turn a turbine and spin an electric generator, and then cooled down in the deep water to be used for another cycle.

Pros	Cons
• Relies on clean and renewable energy source (hydro-thermal power). • Considered to be the largest potential ocean energy. • Compatible with other marine energy such as tidal and wave energy. • Besides energy production, the installation can be used for other activities such as desalination, air conditioning, aquaculture, and mineral extraction etc.	• Currently has only one operating plant in the world (in Japan). • Cost estimates are uncertain since it hasn't been widely deployed. • Needs to be sited in the tropical region (within 20° of the equator), where warm water is layered over cold. • Likely to require high construction and maintenance costs since it relies on long and delicate generators.

Useful references

United Nations' global report on marine-based energy (offshore wind, tide, ocean thermal):

http://www.un.org/depts/los/global_reporting/WOA_RPROC/Chapter_22.pdf

The European Marine Energy Center (wave and tide energy): http://www.emec.org.uk/marine-energy/

Oilscam.org (Infographic on offshore and onshore oil drilling):

http://www.oilscams.org/offshore-vs-onshore-oil-drilling

Sailing Forward   Fishbowl Discussion 1

- A fishbowl discussion is a discussion in which students seating inside the "fishbowl" participate actively in a discussion, while students seating outside listen to the discussion carefully and make observations.
- Five or six volunteered students will seat in a small circle and discuss about what marine-based energy option your local community should support and develop.
    - o One person will be a moderator. The moderator can bring in prompts for discussion and interfere to allocate time equally to all participants.
    - o Each participant supports different marine-based energy source. (One person can oppose all the options, insisting on onshore energy source.)
    - o Participants can use real or imaginary data to support their argument, as long as it doesn't go against our common sense. The suggested data can be counter-argued by opponents.
    - o Be polite to each other, and use **Speaking Tackle 4** on the next page.
    - o Discussion continues for 20 to 25 minutes.
- Students sitting outside the fishbowl will listen to the discussion and take notes.
    - o Which energy option do you support before and after the discussion?
    - o Which argument(s) did you find most persuasive? Why?
    - o Did the participants take turns naturally and effectively? How?
    - o Was there anything that didn't go well in the discussion? How can we modify the rule or set-up for a better discussion?
- As a whole class, students reflect on how they think the discussion went, what you learned from it, and how we can make it better next time.

Speaking Tackle 4 Turn taking in Discussion

- It is important to take a smooth, polite and appropriate turn in discussion. You can do this by using specific phrases or gestures and other body language, and making noises such as 'hmm' and 'ah' while thinking so as to not lose the turn. You can also speak a certain way, for example, using intonation to show that you have or haven't finished and very quickly saying the beginning of your sentence to interrupt.
- There are a few strategies you might consider using in turn taking:
  - First, speak, and then ask.
  - Use conjunctions to add more information for a smooth flow
  - It's also helpful to use phrases for agreeing/disagreeing.
  - Ask for and give opinions of your group members.
  - As mentioned above, use fillers such as 'Let me see...', 'Let me think...', 'What I mean is...' for pauses.

Dive into Grammar

James: I probably made that movie because I believed I could actually dive to the Titanic. And **if I could have** actually **dived** to the Titanic without making the movie, I probably **would have done** that.

As before, we use **if + had (could have) + past perfect** followed by **would/could/might + have + past perfect** to talk about the past wish that did not come true ("counterfactual conditional"). Compare **would (do)** with **would have (done).**

e.g. If I could have actually dived to the Titanic without making the movie, I probably **would be** a diver instead of a filmmaker by now.

Listening Lighthouse

Listen to the news on the first U.S. installation of offshore wind turbine in Rhode Island.

[NPR] Wind of Change? Rhode Island Hopes For First Offshore Wind Farm
https://www.npr.org/2015/08/01/428076271/winds-of-change-rhode-island-hopes-for-first-offshore-wind-farm

Guiding Questions

1. What is happening in Rhode Island?

2. According to Jeff Grybowski, the Chief Executive Officer (C.E.O.) of Deepwater Wind, why has the project in Rhode Island successfully launched, while in Massachusetts, similar project by Cape Wind failed? Identify three reasons.
   1)
   2)
   3)

3. What are the opinions of Block Island residents regarding the offshore wind farm? What do they like or dislike about the offshore wind farm?
   Likes:

   Dislikes:

4. Why all eyes are on Rhode Island's offshore wind farm project in the U.S.?

Extended Listening

Now, watch an extensive report on the Rhode Island offshore wind farm installation.
[PBS] US. Builds First Offshore Wind Farm
https://www.youtube.com/watch?v=rUj0CUlnHhs

1. How are the energy policies in Europe and the U.S. different?

2. Why is there skepticism about the reduced electricity bill when the offshore wind farm is installed?

3. Why do the Block Island residents pay one of the nation's most expensive and unstable electricity rates?

4. According to Kim Gaffett, the former Town Council Leader of Block Island, how will the Block Island residents benefit from the offshore wind farm despite worries about rate increase?

5. What are "floating turbines," proposed by Alla Weinstein? What are the strengths of floating turbines compared to the conventional offshore wind turbines?

• What are your thoughts on relying more on renewable marine energy sources?

The Block Island in Rhode Island (expedia.co.uk)

Chapter 7. Marine Transportation

Chapter Forecast

- In this chapter, you will learn how to consider both pros and cons for a good writing and for a thorough decision-making.
- You will practice how to have a free and open discussion when you are given specific situations and constraints.
- You will observe and learn how people come up with different solutions or conclusions, even with the shared understandings on an issue.

Embark on a Journey Reasons to Cruise

- Watch two videos on Youtube on "reasons (not) to cruse".
  - o 4 Reasons Why You Need To Try a Cruise At Least Once
    https://youtu.be/0gDFLbtz2P8
  - o 5 Reasons to NOT go on a Cruise! https://youtu.be/H8PdtPF0IvM
- In pairs or groups, come up with the reasons to cruise for a vacation.
  - o For how long? To which destination?
  - o What activities would you like to enjoy on a cruise ship?
  - o What concerns do you have?
- Prepare for a discussion for the pros and cons of cruising.
  - o Refer to **Writing Tackle 3** (p. 78) to take two-column notes.
  - o Write a bullet list of pros and cons.

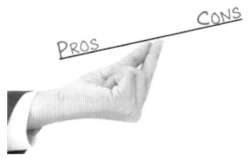

6 Best Cruises for First Timers

Cruising is not the first thing that comes to your mind when you think about traveling because of its limited destinations and faster and accessible alternative transportations. For those who love cruising, however, it offers experiences that nothing else can replace. Look through the following list of recommended cruise lines for first timers and think about which of them interests you most and why.

Contents adapted from https://www.cruisecritic.com/articles.cfm?ID=129

Carnival Cruise Line
Best for: Value hunters
Why: Carnival is intended for "every cruiser," appealing to a broad spectrum of vacationers who share one common trait: They all want a super-fun escape without going bankrupt. With its sizable fleet (25 ships), it disembarks at various popular tourist destinations (Caribbean, Bahamas and Mexico) with three- to seven-night itineraries at affordable prices. Rates typically start around $80 per person, per night, and can be lowered with promotions. Its cabins are simple, but it offers a plenty of onboard venues for fun (e.g. specialty dining venue, serene retreats, comedy clubs) all free of charge. For the best budget rates, avoid holiday periods (especially school vacations).

Royal Caribbean International
Best for: Families with tweens or teens
Why: Older kids need distractions and special attention; Royal Caribbean gives them both. Depending on the ship, the line taps into teens' and tweens' bottomless well of energy with recreations like rock climbing walls, ziplines, ice and inline skating, surf and skydiving simulators, water slides and basketball and volleyball courts. Its youth programs wisely split up tweens and teens into their appropriate age groups. The spa treatments are also designed with sophisticated amenities to accommodate adolescent needs. For thrill

seeking teenagers, it provides multiple outlets such as DJ lessons, teens-only casino nights, backstage tours of the ship, and no-elders-allowed dance lounges with mocktails. The packed schedule, overseen by attentive crew, lets parents enjoy their own downtime without worrying about their near-adult children.

Disney Cruise Line

Best for: Families with small children

Why: Disney really gets what parents and small children need on vacation, from entertainment and dining to childcare. The line is rare in the industry for attending to the needs of babies and toddlers. It provides nurseries for little sailors up to 3 years old and has a pool for diapered babies. The cruise line also fills its ships with its signature characters, such as Mickey, Goofy, Cinderella and her princess pals, who engage youngsters at planned events and spontaneous encounters. Its expansive play areas are themed after popular Disney, Pixar, Star Wars and Marvel movies, with plenty of high-tech games and interactive (and often educational) programs. Cabins and dining establishments are tailored for families, taking into account the practical (split bathrooms with tub/shower combos) and the whimsical (restaurants with fairytale decor).

Paul Gauguin Cruises

Best for: Romantics

Why: Paul Gauguin Cruises offers a singular experience to the ultimate honeymoon, anniversary, special-occasion destinations of French Polynesia and the greater South Pacific. The cabins are designed for perfect romance with great ocean views, queen-sized beds, and private balconies. Couples can feel the ooh-la-la over a Polynesian-accented French meal at the fine-dining restaurant L'Etoile, or during a private sunset dinner served on their stateroom balcony. The spa caters to twosomes with couples' treatments – try the 40-minute aroma steam bath for two or a massage on a private islet off the coast of Taha'a. Plus, the line offers a complimentary package for honeymooners (e.g. an in-room

Champagne toast and a special Polynesian blessing ceremony), as well as a selection of wedding and vow renewal ceremony packages.

Lindblad Expeditions

Best for: Adventurers

Why: Lindblad seeks out exotic itineraries in the Arctic, Antarctica, Galapagos, Amazon and other less-mainstream cruise destinations. On its polar voyages, passengers sail aboard an ice-class vessel that easily slips through frozen passageways populated with polar bears in the Arctic or penguins in Antarctica. Its Torres del Paine-to-Cape Horn itinerary delivers myriad land-and-sea encounters in Patagonia's vast wilderness. On all voyages, passengers can expect to share in the expertise of a team of naturalists, including National Geographic photographers (or Lindblad-National Geographic certified photo instructors) and undersea specialists, providing a steady stream of eco-insights and information. For closer views, the cruise line equips its ships with Zodiacs, sea kayaks, and underwater cameras. Shore excursions are designed for scientific explorations such as naturalist-led glacier hikes and deep-water snorkeling. The company also advances sustainable practices and supports many conservation programs in the fragile destinations it visits.

Norwegian Cruise Line

Best for: Entertainment enthusiasts

Why: All Norwegian ships offer abundant entertainment genres such as musicals, comedy and improv shows, live music and guest performers, but the line really shines with its newest ships: Norwegian Escape, Norwegian Epic, Norwegian Breakaway and Norwegian Getaway. Cruisers can experience Broadway hit musicals like "Rock of Ages," "After Midnight" or "Million Dollar Quartet", sizzling dance shows like "Burn the Floor", comedy by Second City improv or Levity Comedy, and music by dueling pianists and blues bands. The line even turns meals into theater with dinner show Cirque Dreams. Throw in plenty of bars, discos, bowling and Wii, and you will never be bored onboard.

Sailing Forward **Fishbowl Discussion 2**

- This time, you will participate in a fish bowl discussion to account for a variety of situations you may consider cruising.
- Four students will volunteer as discussants for each round of discussion. In total, four rounds of short discussions will take place.
  - o There is no moderator this time. Participants will have a free discussion for 8 minutes whether or not they want to go on a cruise in each scenario.
  - o Discussants do not need to take a side from the beginning, and can change their positions flexibly during the discussion. However, make sure you consider both pros and cons in each discussion.
  - o **Round 1**: You are planning for an island vacation with a group of friends to observe wildlife and enjoy nature. Would you choose a cruise?
  - o **Round 2**: You are planning for a family trip on a beach with seniors and kids. Would you choose a cruise?
  - o **Round 3**: You are planning for a romantic vacation (i.e. honeymoon) as a couple to a popular oceanfront city. Would you choose a cruise?
  - o **Round 4**: You are planning for a travel alone to escape from routines and meet a lot of new people. Would you choose a cruse?
- Students sitting outside the fishbowl will listen to the discussion and fill-in their two-column notes.
  - o For each scenario, mark your preference whether or not to cruise.
  - o For each pro and con bullet point you have written, add supporting arguments or debunk the myths as you listen to the discussions.
  - o Which group do you think took into account both pros and cons in a thorough and balanced manner?
- As a whole class, share your reflections on how the discussions went, what you learned from it, and how we can use discussion for a decision-making.

Writing Tackle 3 Turn Discussion to a Writing

In an argumentative writing, you are asked to take a position or reveal your preference on a controversial issue. However, to take a position does not mean that you can disregard the opposing arguments. The more you know about why and with what grounds others make a different judgment on the same issue, the better you can argue against it. You can also deepen your understandings of an issue by considering different positions, debunking your misconceptions or raising critical questions. Therefore, you can use discussion as a preparation stage for an argumentative writing.

Taking two-column notes during the discussion is an effective way to help identify your misconceptions and questions about a topic, and to account for opposing views through a balanced perspective. Try taking two-column notes while you are observing a discussion as a start. Once you are familiarized with the process, you can use it for your own brainstorming before any kinds of writing.

Steps to use two-column notes

1. Make your notebook or graphic organizer be divided in half with a line or fold.
2. Left side is labeled "Key Ideas", and the right side "Responses". Fill in the left side before listening to a discussion, and fill in the right side as you listen to the discussion.
    a. Key Ideas refer to the main points or main arguments you would like to elaborate.
    b. Responses refer to questions, interpretations, and connections you make from your key ideas.
3. Reflect on your notes to elaborate your position on the issue. Select the points that appeal to you most, and start writing.

Key Ideas	Responses
[Cons] The destination for cruising is rather limited.	NOT if you are looking for a destination rich with wildlife.

Dive into Vocabulary

Search or guess the meanings of vocabulary or phrases below before reading.
While reading, make a better guess of the meanings of vocabulary or phrases.

- ouster (n.) / oust (v.)
- salvage (n.)
- barge (n.)
- bereaved (adj.)
- wreckage (n.)
- consortium (n.)
- semi-submersible vessel
- loophole (n.)
- collude (v.)
- cursory (adj.)
- murder through willful negligence
- botched rescue operation
- grievance (n.)
- blot (n.)
- emblematic (adj.)
- aloofness (n.)
- sweeping (adj.)
- bridge (n.)   the raised part of a ship on which the captain and other officers stand and form where they control the movement of the ship
- be outfitted with
- enclosed lifeboat

Dive into Grammar

Bereaved families have demanded that the ship be salvaged, hoping that the bodies of the missing would be found inside. They also hoped that the wreckage **would reveal** more clues to what caused the ship to sink.

We use **if + past verb** followed by **would/could/might + root verb** to talk about the present wish that may not come true.

Reading Compass

Read the following news on the Sewol Ferry salvage.
[NYT] South Korea Raises Ferry That Sank in 2014 Disaster
https://www.nytimes.com/2017/03/22/world/asia/south-korea-ferry-sewol.html

Guiding Questions

1. According to the article, why did the families of the Sewol Ferry victims demanded the ship be salvaged?

2. What were the roles of barges and a semi-submersible vessel in the salvage operation?

3. What loopholes in safety standards did the investigation of the sinking reveal?
   1)
   2)
   3)
   4)

4. According to the article, why did many South Koreans blame the former President Park Geun-hye after the Sewol Ferry accident?

Reading Compass

Expand Your Reading

Now, listen to the news on the National Transportation Safety Board's report on the El Faro accident.

[NPR] NTSB Shares Recommendations For Maritime Shipping Industry In El Faro Report

https://www.npr.org/2017/12/12/570248517/ntsb-shares-recommendations-for-maritime-shipping-industry-in-el-faro-report

1. What happened to the cargo ship El Faro in 2015?

2. Why did the El Faro's captain go directly into the path of the storm?
1)
2)
3)

3.What did the NTSB suggest to have caused the tragic accident?
1)
2)
3)

- Based on the two ship wrecking accidents, what roles do you think the government should play to ensure the safety of marine transportation?

Chapter 8. Maritime History

Chapter Forecast

- In this chapter, you will learn how to write an online review on a blog with style and manner.
- You will collect materials for writings through virtual or actual museum visits.
- You will expand your understanding on a reading by referring to various online media and materials—videos, photos, and texts.

Embark on a Journey **Maritime Superstars**

- In pairs or groups, talk about your favorite historical figure(s) related to the maritime history.
  - o Which era did the person(s) live?
  - o What did the person(s) do? What made him/her/them famous?
  - o What do you think the person(s) have contributed to the maritime history?
- One person in each team will share their discussion with the whole class, focusing on the question "what are the common traits of the historical figures who were considered superstars in maritime history?"

Maritime Museums around the World

Maritime museums play an important role in presenting noteworthy marine artifacts and educating the visitors of remarkable marine events. Around the world, there are many maritime museums established with different focuses, i.e. ships and ship-making, naval and marine wars, marine resources, marine art and culture etc. This variety in their themes shows that human beings have explored the oceans through so many activities and unfolded diverse stories. Search on the web about the characteristics and collections of maritime museums around the world, and you will learn a lot about how people in each city and country have been developing their relationships with the oceans.

List of major maritime museums: https://en.wikipedia.org/wiki/Maritime-museum

National Maritime Museum, Greenwich, London, UK

Considered to be one of the finest and largest museums of its kind, the museum is housed in the Maritime Greenwich World Heritage Site. It was founded in 1934 as Royal Museums Greenwich and changed to its current name in 2012. As Greenwich is the birthplace of longitude and has been historically associated with the sea and navigation, the major collections include instruments for early astronomical studies, navigation, and time measurement. It also has abundant maritime art pieces, cartography, manuscripts, ship models and plans.

Website: https://www.rmg.co.uk/national-maritime-museum

Australian National Maritime Museum, Sydney, AU

Located in Darling Harbour, Sydney, the museum is the symbol of Australia's ongoing passion for modernity and redevelopment. The museum opened in 1991 in the building designed by Philip Cox. It consists of seven main galleries for permanent exhibits and four additional galleries for temporary exhibits. The permanent exhibits deal with discovery of Australia, Australian Aborigines' relationships with the water, journeys made to Australia by settlers and other groups, water recreation and entertainment, Royal Australian Navy, and Australia-US relationship. There are also three museum ships open to public inspection and other vessels on display.

Website: http://www.anmm.gov.au/visit/visit

Maritime Museum of San Diego, San Diego, California, USA

Established in 1948, the museum has one of the largest collections of historic sea vessels in the U.S. In fact, the vessels serve as the museum buildings. Its centerpiece, *Star of India* is a merchant bark built in 1863, and has sailed from Great Britain to India and New Zealand, became a salmon hauler in the U.S., retired in 1926, and now is serving as a floating gallery. The museum's other building, 1898 *Berkeley* has the MacMullen Library and Research Archives on board. The museum supports academic research on sea vessels, publishing the quarterly journal *Mains'l Haul: A Journal Of Pacific Maritime History*.

Website: https://sdmaritime.org/

The Netherlands National Maritime Museum, Amsterdam, Netherlands

The museum is housed in a formal naval storehouse, which was constructed in 1656 and became the museum building gin 1973. Its interior has been fully renovated and reopened in 2011, adding the glass roof of the courtyard inspired by the compass rose on nautical maps.

Outside the building, a replica of the *Amsterdam* is moored outside the museum, an 18th century ship that sailed between the Netherlands and the East Indies. The collections include artifacts related to shipping and sailing, paintings, cartography, scale models, and weapons from the 17th century, which was called the Golden Age of the Netherlands. For example, the museum displays life and artifacts of Jan Janszoon Weltevree, who became one of the first Europeans to set foot in Korea.

Website: https://www.hetscheepvaartmuseum.nl/

Kobe Maritime Museum, Kobe, Japan
The museum opened in 1987 to celebrate the 120th anniversary of the Port of Kobe, which now has become one of the busiest international ports in Japan. The museum offers a glimpse at ship making, port facilities, and latest cruise ships through which the visitors can learn the history and predict the future of the ships, ports, and seas. It also offers many interactive learning experiences such as handling actual navigation instruments, taking a look at ship records, diorama models, graphics, and watching videos on ships, ports, and the seas. A part of the earthquake-damaged Meriken wharf is also preserved as the Port of Kobe Earthquake Memorial Park to pass on the lessons learned from the earthquake to the next generation.

Website: http://www.kobe-maritime-museum.com/language/english.html

Korea National Maritime Museum, Busan, South Korea
The museum was inaugurated in 2012 at Yeongdo-gu, Busan, right next to the International Cruise Terminal and near Korea Maritime and Ocean University. The museum is equipped with high tech facilities including interactive Children's Museum, Science Hall, and 4D Theater. Its collections range from a half size replica of Joseon Missional Ship to the latest deep sea and polar region exploring devices. The visitors can learn various human activities took place on the ocean from 5,000 years ago to present. The museum also aims to spread environmental perspectives on marine industry and educate the importance of marine preservation.

Website: http://www.knmm.or.kr/eng/main/main.aspx

Sailing Forward Visiting Maritime Museums

- In a team or individually, you will plan for a virtual or actual visit to a maritime museum.
  - o Write a short introductory passage about the general characteristics of the museum (history, location, themes, and major collections). Also write you chose to visit the museum.

  - o Study what permanent and temporary exhibitions are taking place, and choose one or two exhibition(s) that you are most interested in.

- [Homework] Make a virtual or actual visit to a maritime museum of your choice. Take notes of your impressions about the organization, exhibits, activities, and other aspects of the museum. Then,
  - o Write a review on a blog of the maritime museum—it can be a holistic review or a focused review that only talks about one or few collection(s). In any case, include an introductory passage and general information (location, admission, operating hours, etc.) for visitors.

  - o Refer to **Writing Tackle 4** for tips to write a helpful review online.

  - o Students are encouraged to present their work next week, focusing on what you've learned and felt.

Writing Tackle 4 Writing Reviews on a Blog

Let's face it. Most of us spend less time reading physical books than reading online materials these days. It is pointless to deny the usefulness of online materials in the modern life.

Among many forms of online materials, we get to read a lot of online reviews. People value personal reviews because of its honesty and accessibility. Since they are based on a personal perspective and typically tailored for readers with shared interests, you can find information that better serves your needs with a right search.

If you love reading online reviews, why don't you try writing one yourself and share your experience? Here are some hands-on tips to write a helpful online review.

1. Honesty is the Key

People search for reviews before they invest their money and time on something to see if it is worth trying. The most helpful reviews are the ones written and maintained by ordinary people who have real-life experience with the product or service. So it helps to write the review from your own perspective, rather than what you heard or read about the product or service.

Say you are writing about maritime museum, make it tangible to the readers who you are (age, interest...) and why you visited the place. Follow a simple format of:
- Short intro to the maritime museum (its aims, location, hours, admission...)
- What you liked and disliked about the museum or its exhibits (in a balanced manner, if possible)
- What was your purpose of visiting, and whether it's been met or not
- Advice or comments to the potential visitors

2. Using Photos and Images

You should include some unique photos or images of the product or service to give a real sense of it, and to prove that you've actually experienced it. Make sure to take photos clear and interesting.

When you are taking photos at the museum, beware that photograph is now allowed in some sections. Take photos at the entrance or with the museum's signature symbols at the open square. If photograph is allowed for some of the exhibits, take a few photos without disturbing the gallery's atmosphere.

If you need to use someone else's photos for your review, make sure you are using them legally. Search for open source photos in places like *Creative Commons*, or cite the photo properly with a permission of the creator. Remember that it is absolutely important to keep the public manners when you are posting online publicly.

3. Disclaimer Statement

A disclaimer explains the connection or relationship between a company or brand and a blog owner. Because many companies and brands these days provide payments or free products and services to the bloggers for advertisement, the Fair Trade Commission requires bloggers to indicate explicitly when they are writing reviews in return for compensations.

If you paid for the product or service, you are not required to put a disclaimer, but many blogs choose to have a short disclaimer at the bottom of their posts to make sure that it is a personally motivated review.

4. Sharing on Social Media

Once you have posted a review on your blog, you can consider promoting it through social media such as *Facebook, Twitter, Instagram,* or *Pinterest*. Not only will your regular visitors read your blog, but also a larger community on social media will check on your blog and make a personal bond with you.

One word of caution to keep in mind is not to become a spammer. Posting your reviews randomly on social media can be considered spamming by some. Therefore, you should sparingly re-share your review post with different wordings, which can appeal to different groups of audience. Also, be consistent in social media when expressing your interests in certain themes or topics to be considered an honest and reliable reviewer.

Dive into Vocabulary

Search or guess the meanings of vocabulary or phrases below before reading. While reading, make a better guess of the meanings of vocabulary or phrases.

- the Longitude Act
- tormented (adj.)
- a Rake's Progress (by William Hogarth)
- hack draftsman
- chronometer (n.)
- obsolete (v.)
- the cascade effect
- sextant (n.)
- observatory (n.)
- luminary (n.)
- Captain Cook (or Captain James Cook)
- HMS Bounty (HMS: Her/His Majesty's Ship)
- mutiny (n.)

Dive into Grammar

He got most of the details, but the debate about it has already moved on: **the unfortunate** is now agonizing about clockwork mechanisms, and has written "the clock does strike by algebra".

As shown in the above sentence, the structure **'the + adjective'** is used to talk about some well-known groups of people. Some common examples are: the blind, the deaf, the unemployed, the rich, the young, the old, and the dead.
  - Bill is collecting money for the blind. (= He is collecting money for blind people.)
  - The charity group should do something for the poor.
Note that these expressions are always plural. The blind means all blind people. Adjectives are not normally used in this way without 'the'.

Read the following article on Harrison's sea clock and the Longitude Act.
[The Guardian] Maritime museum finds time for celebration of Harrison's sea clock
https://www.theguardian.com/culture/2014/jul/09/ships-clocks-stars-longi
tude-act-maritime-museum-harrison-anniversary

Guiding Questions

1. What were on show in a new exhibition at the Maritime Museum in Greenwich?

2. What was the difference between the two prints?

3. What did the draftsman and the public at that time know about so-called "the problem of longitude"?

4. According to the curator Richard Dunn, why would John Harrison's marine chronometer still be useful in modern times?

5. Why was the Longitude Act established in 1714?

6. How would you summarize John Harrison's contribution to the maritime history?

Reading Compass

Expand Your Reading

Now, watch part of the following documentary on Harrison's clock to understand deeper how it helped maritime navigation.

[BBC] The Clock that Changed the World (BBC History of the World)
https://youtu.be/T-g27KS0yiY [20:37-23:42]

1. What mechanism did Harrison use on his clock to keep it accurate while ship is severely rocking?

2. When and how did Harrison eventually get the prize for solving the Longitude problem?

Visit the virtual gallery of the exhibition featuring the Longitude Act and also watch an introductory video on the same exhibition when it toured the U.S.

[The Guardian] Ships, Clocks & Stars: new exhibition—in pictures
https://www.theguardian.com/science/the-h-word/gallery/2014/jul/10/ships-clocks-stars-exhibition-in-pictures

[The Guardian] The Greenwich longitude exhibition on tour
https://www.theguardian.com/science/the-h-word/2015/oct/05/longitude-exhibition-tour-history-science

• Which artifact(s) did you find most interesting? Why do you think it is important to preserve maritime artifacts and educate maritime history?

Chapter 9. Marine Sports and Sports Fishing

Chapter Forecast

- In this chapter, you will learn how to give and receive feedback on your oral presentation.
- You will practice how to share your opinion in a pair or small group, as well as in a whole class setting.
- You will learn practical tips to understand a short interview in a radio – by finding out key words and identifying a main sentence.

Embark on a Journey **Introducing Marine Sports**

• In pairs or groups, choose one water sport you like to play or would like to try on a sea, and talk about:
    o Why you like (to try) the sport,
    o Where is the best place / when is the best season to enjoy the sport,
    o What equipment you need,
    o To what group of people you would recommend the sport,
    o Key safety rules.
• Prepare a short presentation of your pair/group work and present it to the whole class with a theme "Best marine sport you should try".
o Among the audience, 3 students will volunteer to provide a written feedback on each presentation. The rest will listen to the presentation, and freely ask questions. For tips to giving and receiving peer feedback on speech, refer to **Speaking Tackle 5** (p. 100).
o Share some of the common issues found during presentation and find out solutions through a whole-class discussion. Discuss what the skills are to give a clear and helpful feedback.

Top 10 Marine Sports You Should Try

Refer to *The Guardian* "Top 10 water sports and activities in Tobago" for vivid examples:
https://www.theguardian.com/travel/2013/oct/01/top-10-water-sports-activities-tobago

Sailing

Sailing is one of the oldest forms of marine transportations, but has become recreation or sports in recent days. Recreational sailing can be divided into racing and cruising. Through racing, you can enjoy the power of wind at the full speed, while cruising allows you to interact with marine life and enjoy great views.

Equipment: a sailboat, drysuits/rashguards/technical apparel, a life jacket, sunglasses, a watch, a marine VHF radio set, etc.

Kitesurfing

Kitesurfing refers to wave riding using a board towed by a large controllable power kite. The rider can control the direction of the kite with a control bar. A harness, which comes in various types, spreads the kite's pull across the rider's body and enables the rider to perform jumps or other hands-free movements.

Equipment: a surfboard or kiteboard, a kite, a harness, a control bar, boots, foot straps, wetsuits/rashguards, a floatation vest, etc.

Scuba Diving

Scuba diving is underwater diving wearing a self-contained underwater breathing device (scuba), which gives a diver greater independence and freedom of movement than surface-supplied devices. Depending on the temperature of water you'd like to dive, you need to prepare different types of scuba gears.

Equipment: a scuba tank, a regulator, dive computers, submersible pressure gauge (SPG), a mask, a snorkel, fins, a buoyance control device (BCD), wetsuits/dry suits/body suits, dive light, dive knife, safety gears, etc.

Snorkeling

Snorkeling is shallow water swimming with light equipment including a shaped breathing tube called snorkel. Snorkel is suitable to observe underwater attractions for extended period with relatively little skill. Since anyone who has basic swimming skills can enjoy it, it is popular recreational activity recommended for family travelers, particularly at tropical resort locations.

Equipment: a diving mask, a snorkel, swimsuits, fins, etc.

Windsurfing

Windsurfing is a combination of surfing and sailing. Standing on a 2.5 to 3-meter long board connected to a rig (consists of a mast and sail), the rider can windsurf by controlling the boom (bar) attached to the sail. Windsurfing has been recognized as an Olympic sport since 1984 as "sailing".

Equipment: a sail, a mast, a board, foot straps, barefoot shoes, wetsuits/rashguards/swimsuits, sunglasses, etc.

Parasailing

Parasailing is a recreational kiting in which a person is towed behind a motorboat while attached to a specially designed parachute. When the vehicle drives off and reaches a good speed, it sends a person carrying the wing into the air. The parascender has little or no control over the parachute. If the motorboat is powerful enough, two or three people can parasail at the same time.

Equipment: a motorboat, a harness, a tandem, risers, lines, a parasail canopy, parasail ropes, parasail winch, a life jacket, etc.

Sea Kayaking

Sea kayaking is using a kayak developed for paddling on open waters like the sea. The hull comes in a wide range of designs and lengths, which determines its range of performance. Typically, shorter boats are easier to control, whereas longer boats travel straighter and faster. Some kayaks are designed for more than one person.

Equipment: a kayak, paddles, personal flotation device (PFD), tow systems, a spray skirt, wetsuits/dry suits, a GPS unit, etc.

Surfing

Surfing is wave riding which carries the surfer towards the shore. Because it requires relatively big and regular waves (or swells) than other water sports, surfers need to search for the best locations and seasons for surfing in advance. Surfing has been newly recognized as an Olympic sport starting from 2020.

Equipment: a surfboard, fins, a leash, wetsuits/rashguards, water shoes, webbed gloves, a hood, etc.

Wakeboarding

Wakeboarding is riding of a wakeboard on the surface of the water toed behind a motorboat. The rider demonstrates various jumps and tricks that are derived from water skiing, snowboarding, and surfing. Since the rider has to tolerate the pull only through arms, it requires strong arms as well as good balancing skills.

Equipment: a motorboat, a wakeboard, boots, foot straps, helmet, buoyance aid, wetsuits/rashguards/swimsuits, etc.

Stand Up Paddling

Stand up paddling is a kind of surfing using a paddle. Because it can be performed in relatively calm and placid water, it is suitable for first-time surfers or people who wish to enjoy mild surfing. As its popularity increases, many variations including paddle board yoga, fitness, and fishing are also attracting people.

Equipment: a stand up paddle board, a paddle, personal flotation device (PFD), a safety whistle, rashguards/swimsuits, sunglasses etc.

Sailing Forward Water Sport Dos and Don'ts

- [Pair/Group] The following sentences are taken from the list of safety rules that the Leisure and Cultural Services Department of Hong Kong has suggested. Read the sentences and categorize them to dos or don'ts. (See the full list at: http://www.lcsd.gov.hk/en/watersport/guideline/guid_safety.html)

Behavior	Do/ Don't
Conduct water sports activities in the same waters with high-speed boats.	
Acquire basic swimming skills and be able to swim at least 50 meters with clothes.	
Inform reliable people of your destination, time of return journey and ways of contact with your companions.	
Conduct capsize training in waters with unknown depth.	
Keep clear of the navigation waterway, mooring area, and fishing boats.	
Overload and randomly adjust the pre-set devices in the boat.	
Conduct activities under poor visibility, rapid current or offshore strong wind without any shelter.	
Wear heel-toe covered rubber shoes, clothes suitable for water sports such as swimming suits, sun cap, light, permeable, and fit long-sleeves	
Take part in water sports activities with companions and look after one another.	
Overrate your skills and physical strength to show superiority.	

- ❖ [Follow-up] This week, students are encouraged to present their blog posts on maritime museums.
  - o Give a 5-minute presentation to the class about your visit focusing on what you've learned and felt.
  - o The audience will take notes of what the presenter did well and what can be improved. Each student will provide feedback to (pre-assigned) three groups or individuals. Refer to **Speaking Tackle 5** (p. 100) for tips to give feedback to your colleagues.

Speaking Tackle 5　Giving and Getting Peer Feedback

Peer feedback provides a bilateral opportunity for students to learn from each other. Students who give feedback can recognize their peer's mistake and reflect on their own knowledge and performance. Students who receive feedback can hear frank opinions from someone who is at a similar level of learning, and think about their own strengths and weaknesses.

However, for peer feedback to have positive impact on learning, students should be able to respect and trust each other. Those who provide feedback need to embrace the difficulties and anxiety of the presenter during a public speech, and try to point out their weakness and your advice with approachable and understandable language, using specific examples. Those who receive feedback need to value their peers' feedback because they provided care and efforts in providing it. Although some of the responses may not look clear or feel just, but try to embrace it as one genuine reaction from learners at similar learning stages.

One way to provide more constructive and helpful feedback is to use the rubrics through which you can visualize and quantify your responses. Following is an example of the rubrics you can use when giving feedback on speech. Take a look, and think about various aspects of speech. If possible, what element(s) would you add on to the table?

Requirement	4　Very good	3 Good	2 Can be improved	1 Needs work
Appropriateness of content and target audience	*Write examples & specific advice*			
Coherence of the speech structure				
Engagement of the audience (visuals, evidence, style)				
Management of the presentation (time, voice)				
Clarity in the use of language (word, grammar)				
Totals:	Overall opinion:			

Dive into Vocabulary

Search or guess the meanings of vocabulary or phrases below before listening. While listening, make a better guess of the meanings of vocabulary or phrases.

- red snapper (n.)
- marina (n.)
- vermilion (n.)
- fillet (n.)
- take advantage of ~
- cross the line
- fishery (n.)
- a quota system
- angler (n.)
- for-hire (adj.)
- charter boat
- contentious (adj.)
- litigation (n.)
- a fair shake
- write a check
- a short-term fix
- in exchange for ~
- representative (vs. senator)
- "the issue has been mounting"
- electrify (v.)
- bottom feeder
- bill oneself as ~
- overrule (v.)
- precedent (n.)
- decimate (v.)
- do away with ~
- oversight
- livelihood (n.)

Dive into Grammar

The fishery has become an economic engine for Orange Beach, **which** bills itself as the red snapper capital of the world.

Ard is on the board of the national Charter Fishermen's Association, **which** calls the action a dangerous precedent that could lead to overfishing and stricter quota for everybody next year under federal law.

In the above example sentence, ", which…." or the relative clauses give us extra information about the person or thing. We use commas (,) with these clauses. Look at the following example sentence:

My sister Jennifer, **who** lives in New York, is a nurse.

Listening Lighthouse

Listen to the news on conflicts around the recreational red snapper catch in the Gulf of Mexico.

[NPR] Who gets to fish for red snapper in the Gulf? It's all politics
https://www.npr.org/sections/thesalt/2017/07/07/535021139/who-gets-to-fish-for-red-snapper-in-the-gulf-its-all-politics
Transcripts
https://www.npr.org/templates/transcript/transcript.php?storyId=535021139

Guiding Questions

1. How long was the recreational red snapper season initially this year? How has it been extended?

2. Why did the federal government start to regulate the red snapper catch? How did the fed set a quota system?

Listening Lighthouse

3. What was the consequence of the federal government's regulation on the recreational fishermen group?

4. Why are the local (state) governments in conflict with the federal government with regard to snapper management? What do the state governments want?

5. Who (or which group) is unsatisfied with overruling of regulations? Why?

Personal Take

• Summarize the argument of each stakeholder that appears in this article. Identify their priority and attitude towards red snapper management.
  o Private anglers:

  o Commercial fishermen:

  o The federal government:

  o The state government(s):

• Put yourself in one of the stakeholders' shoes (it can be someone who doesn't appear on the news), and write a letter either to the government or the public. What would you argue about red snapper management? What is your priority?

Chapter 10. Tastes of the Sea

Chapter Forecast

- In this chapter, you will learn how to deliver your cultural understanding and practical knowledge to the global audience by making a seafood recipe video.
- You will practice how to utilize multimedia tools to provide multimodal inputs and promote others' understanding.
- You will learn how to paraphrase and summarize other's writings and incorporate them into your own writing.

Embark on a Journey Favorite Seafood Recipe

- In pairs or groups, choose one of your favorite seafood dishes and write down a recipe for the global audience. The dish can be local or foreign, but make sure you know well enough about the dish to explain cultural backgrounds and know how to make it "delicious".
  - o How would you translate its name in English (if necessary)?
  - o What ingredients and tools do you need?
  - o In what orders do you cook the ingredients, for how long?
  - o Are there any secret tips to make it extra delicious?
- Test the recipe step-by-step virtually, and present it in front of the class to ask for feedback. Refer to **Speaking Tackle 5** (p. 100) for tips to giving and receiving feedback on speech.

How To Write an Easy-to-Follow Recipe

Seemingly a simple task, it requires an art to making a recipe easy to follow. A small mistake can cause confusions like using the wrong measurement or using unclear terms for cooking. So choose each word carefully, use visual aids effectively, and test your instructions step by step before sharing with others. Here are some tips on how to write an elegant recipe that can appeal to the broad audience.

Contents adapted from https://www.wikihow.com/Write-a-Recipe

Setting Up

- Conceptualize your recipe considering the target audience, their cooking style, and the skill level. Is it intended for local or global audience? How familiar are the audience with Korean dishes? Are you targeting a beginner or an experienced cook?

- Consider your purpose of sharing the recipe: if you'd like to prioritize accessibility and generalizability or if you'd rather focus on authenticity and personal touches to the dish.

- Gather all the ingredients required to make your recipe. Are all the ingredients easy to buy at the local or international grocery stores? Also, don't forget to include water, ice, and other essential ingredients.

- Gather your supplies needed to make the dish. Do you need a special pan or pot, bowl, spatula, cooking chopsticks or any other equipment? You may need to provide alternative options and ideas to replace special tools to make the recipe more accessible.

- Imagine that you're cooking a dish for the first time and cook in your thoughts. Divide the stages roughly to the prep work, heating/cooking, and garnishing/decorating. As you go through, take notes on what you do, paying attention to measurements and ingredients. Pay attention to the use of exact cooking and baking terminology. Consider when will be the best time to take photos.

Listing the Ingredients

- Provide exact measurements and volumes for each ingredient. Indicate units clearly (imperial, metric, or both), and use consistent abbreviations (e.g. tsp for teaspoon, tbs for tablespoon).
- List ingredients in the order of your use. This makes easier for the reader to keep track of which ingredients have been used. If they are used together, list them in order of volume.
- Consider readability by breaking the list into more than one part, if necessary. For example, if it has two or more components, such as the dish and sauce, divide the ingredient list with appropriate titles such as "For the dish" and "For the sauce". If there is one ingredient used in multiple steps, then write "divided". (e.g. ½ cup green onion, divided)
- Include techniques in the ingredient list can be helpful. To make your recipe less wordy, you can include simple techniques like *chopped, minced, melted, sliced* as part of the ingredient list. (e.g. 1 tablespoon butter, melted)

Writing the Method

- Describe the equipment needed. Be specific about the size, shape, and composition of the supplies (e.g. a 20cm stone-pot) to guide your readers as carefully as possible.
- Write clear, easy-to-read descriptions of the process. Break it down into simple steps and use common cooking or baking terminology. Long, complicated explanations can be added in a separate paragraph to make the method easy to follow.
- Indicate cooking temperatures (e.g. medium high, medium low) and times. If you cannot determine the time exactly, give hints about how the food should look, smell, and feel like. (e.g. Boil until the fish becomes tender, about 15 minutes.)
- Describe how to finish the dish. Serving is just as important as cooking, so indicate how it needs to be served. (e.g. Serve in the pot and prepare individual dishes. / Let it cool for 10 minutes before serving.)

Adding Final Touches

- Title the recipe to attract people. Give a brief but appetizing description. (e.g. Sweet and Sour Chicken Soup, Mom Made Pickles)

- Consider giving a short introduction. Does your recipe have a history or personal story you'd like to introduce? What occasions make you miss the food? Build a rapport with the audience before presenting the recipe.
- Provide helpful information. For example, how many servings will the recipe provide? How long are the prep and cooking time? Is there any ingredient that may cause allergic reactions? Any warnings about expected problems? (e.g. Do not let the empty clay-pot gets overheated. It may break.)
- Review and revise the organization, composition, and placement of photos/visual aids. Typically, recipes follow the order of: Title, Introduction, Ingredient list, Method, Number of servings, Cooking time.

Seafood Recipes

Here go a couple of examples of delectable seafood recipes and links to recipe videos!

Korean Abalone Porridge
Jeonbokjuk 전복죽

Find out more detailed instructions and a recipe video at:
https://www.maangchi.com/recipe/jeonbokjuk

Ingredients (2-3 servings)
- 2 fresh medium sized abalones (or 4 to 5 ounces of frozen abalone)
- 1 cup rice, rinsed and soaked in cold water for 1 hour
- 2 tsp sesame oil
- 2 garlic cloves, minced
- 5-6 cups of water
- ⅓ cup chopped carrot
- 2 to 3 chopped green onions
- 1 tsp fish sauce
- 1 tsp salt
- eggs (optional)
- 1 sheet of seaweed paper toasted, and crushed

Preparation
Clean abalones
1. Scrub the tops and sides of the abalone with a clean kitchen brush or sponge and salt.
2. Cut off the tip.
3. If they are still in the shells, gently and firmly pry them out with a spoon. Remove the intestines, too.
4. Wash and scrub the meat and intestines in clean running water.

Directions
Make porridge
1. Soak rice for 1 hour before cooking.
2. Heat the sesame oil in a deep pan or pot and gently stir-fry the abalone.
3. Next, add the rice and 6 cups of water and bring to a boil.
4. Reduce the heat when it comes to a boil and then cover the pan.

Spicy Seafood Stew
Haemultang 해물탕

Find out an alternative recipe at:
https://www.koreanbapsang.com/2016/02/
haemul-jeongol-spicy-seafood-hot-pot.html

Ingredients (4 servings)
- 2 octopuses (500g)
- 1 blue crab
- 4 shrimps (100g)
- 8 littleneck clams
- 8 mussels
- 120g radish
- 90g bean sprouts
- 90g oyster mushrooms
- 90g water parsley (or crown daisy)
- 2 green chili peppers
- pinch of salt

Broth: 1.5L water, 8 clams, 8 mussels, 2 tbsp soup soy sauce, pinch of salt

Marinade: 3 tbsp red chili pepper flakes, 1 tbsp red chili paste, 1 tbsp soybean paste, 4 tbsp water, ½ tbsp crushed garlic, 1 tbsp soup soy sauce, 1tsp ginger juice, 2 tbsp *cheongju* or cooking rice wine, pinch of salt

Preparation
Trim ingredients
1. Wash clams and mussels. Boil in a pot with six cups of cold water. Shake dry after boiling. Pour stock into a bowl to separate from sand at the bottom.
2. Brush clean the blue crab. Divide body into four chunks.
3. Separate ink sac from octopus. Massage with 1 tsp salt and rinse in cold water. Cut into strips about 4 to 5 cm long.
4. Scoop out shrimps after rinsing in salt water.
5. From the marinade, mix remaining ingredients in red chili pepper flakes.

Directions
Make stew
1. Lay radish and bean sprouts on the bottom of a wide, shallow pot. Add blue crabs, octopuses, shrimps, clams, and mussels. Pour marinade over ingredients.
2. Season clam stock with salt and soup soy sauce. Pour into shallow pot and boil over medium heat until radish and seafood are cooked.
3. Add water parsley, mushrooms, and chili pepper. Boil for three more minutes.
4. Serve in the pot with individual bowls for sharing.

Sailing Forward Seafood Recipe Video

- Make a 3-minute video of the seafood you would like to share with the international audience.
  - o Introduce the food's native name and translate it to English for understanding.
  - o Explain the food's taste and origin briefly.
  - o Introduce ingredients at the beginning.
  - o Introduce the recipe with relevant pictures or videos for each step.
  - o Show the completed dish and add final comments.

Video Making Tool

For a complete newbie to video making and editing, there are a lot of open-sourced online editing tools available. "Wevideo" is one of such tools, which allows you to add edit photos or video clips, add background music, narrations, sound effects, and subtitles easily. Go to www.wevideo.com

Writing Tackle 5 Paraphrasing and Summarizing

Whether you are writing for fun or for academic purposes, you will need to search and incorporate others' writing into your own texts. Two key skills you can utilize are paraphrasing and summarizing. Paraphrasing refers to changing the language and structure into your own whereas summarizing refers to getting rid of details and leaving the main points. These skills are needed mainly for three reasons. First, while changing and incorporating the language of the original writing, you can enrich your understanding and make ideas your own. Second, you can adapt the contents and language choices to meet the needs of your target audience. Third, you can avoid plagiarism, which is copying the original author's intellectual property without giving credit or obtaining permission.

Paraphrasing and summarizing may look like similar skills, and they are often used together. Think on your own how two skills are different, and how you would use them differently in your own writing.

Paraphrasing

Paraphrasing is rewriting of a sentence with different language or structure. When you are using someone else's sentence in your own writing, but don't want to quote it directly, you paraphrase it. You should keep the ideas same, but changes the words to synonyms or the arrangement of words using different structure/grammar. The benefit of paraphrasing is that you are able to incorporate someone else's idea in details without harming the flow of your own text.

<u>Example</u>

Original sentence:

Illegal fishing, some fear, has the potential to unmoor diplomatic relations.

Paraphrase:

Some people fear that fishing illegally may unsettle diplomatic relations.

Writing Tackle 5

Summarizing

Summarizing is a compact version of a longer original writing. When you'd like to present only the main points of someone else's writing, but don't want to mention the details, you can summarize. You should distinguish the main idea from subsidiary ideas in the original writing by grasping the keywords and essential logic. The benefit of summarizing is that you are able to transform a large amount of information in a short and concise text, which only includes the essence of the original writing. Whether you want to support your idea with other's argument or dispute someone else's argument, summarizing is a useful skill.

Example
Original text:

Some authorities in the Pacific region have responded aggressively to illegal fishing. In September, three Chinese fishermen were killed in a boat fire near South Korea. According to local reports, South Korean maritime police threw flash grenades into the boat after it ignored a warning. The police said the boat was suspected of illegal fishing.

South Korea said in early October that it would use greater force in dealing with Chinese boats fishing illegally in its waters, including shooting at them. It recently summoned China's ambassador to protest an incident in which a South Korean coast guard vessel was rammed by a Chinese boat that was allegedly fishing illegally. South Korea told the ambassador that the incident was "a challenge to public power."

Summary:

Conflicts are rising in the Pacific region due to illegal fishing as the recent South Korea's fire-armed responses to Chinese illegal fishing boats shows. These also resulted in aggravated diplomatic relations between China and South Korea.

Search or guess the meanings of vocabulary or phrases below before reading. While reading, make a better guess of the meanings of vocabulary or phrases.

- state banquet
- trilateral (adj.)
- simmer (v.)
- opt for ~
- fare (n.) e.g. US-style fare of cheeseburgers and steak
- fermented (adj.)
- sole (n.)
- dried persimmon
- eave (n.)
- denuclearisation (n.) or denuclearization

Dive into Grammar

One of Mr. Trump's goal on his 12-day trip to Asia is to boost trilateral cooperation between the US, South Korea, and Japan, **who** are both key allies in countering the nuclear missile threat from North Korea despite simmering diplomatic tensions between them.

This morning I met Jason, **whom** I hadn't seen for years.

We stayed at the Urban Paradise Hotel, **which** a friend of ours recommended.

As shown in the above example sentences, the relative clauses here give us extra information about the person or thing.

Reading Compass

Read the news article on the state banquet when Donald Trump visited South Korea.

[The Telegraph] Politics on the menu in Seoul as Donald Trump dines on shrimp from disputed waters and 360-year-old soy sauce

https://www.telegraph.co.uk/news/2017/11/07/politics-menu-seoul-donald-trump-dines-shrimp-disputed-waters/

Guiding Questions

1. According to the article, why did the menu served at the state banquet become an issue?

2. How was the meal served to Donald Trump in Tokyo similar or different from the meal served in Seoul? In your opinion, what difference(s) in meaning do the meals convey?

Reading to Writing

- [Paraphrase] Paraphrase the following sentence in your own words. Use tips from **Writing Tackle 5** (pp. 113-114).

Original:

International politics will literally be on the menu during US President Donald Trump's visit to South Korea on Tuesday, after it was revealed that shrimp caught in disputed waters will be served up at a state banquet in Seoul.

Paraphrase:

Reading Compass

- [Summarize] Summarize the following paragraphs into one or two sentences. Use tips from **Writing Tackle 5** (pp. 113-114).

Original:

The menu for the four-course state banquet on Tuesday night features shrimp caught in waters off Dokdo, islands controlled by South Korea that are also claimed by Japan (where they are called Takeshima). In a further provocation, one attendee will be a woman forced to work as a sex slave for the Japanese military during World War II.

One of Trump's goals on the trip was to boost trilateral cooperation between the U.S., Japan and South Korea in the face of threats from North Korean leader Kim Jong Un and China's growing dominance in the Asia-Pacific region. Yet cooperation could once more be hindered by historical grievances stemming from Japan's colonial occupation of the Korean peninsula from 1910 to 1945. (Taken from https://www.bloomberg.com/news/articles/2017-11-07/subtle-digs-at-japan-on-the-menu-at-banquet-for-trump-in-seoul)

Summary:

- Write about a seafood cuisine that carries a special cultural/historical meaning to you and your community. Use paraphrasing or summarizing to incorporate other's idea.
  - o Write a topic sentence. (e.g. "No matter what culture, everywhere around the world, people get together to eat." – A quote from Guy Fieri)
  - o Elaborate on the topic using your own example.

Chapter 11. Restoring Marine Environment

Chapter Forecast

- In this chapter, you will learn how to organize your speech into an effective opening, followed by a body, and a closing.
- You will practice how to share your opinion in a pair or small group, as well as in a whole class setting.
- You will learn practical tips to understand a short interview in a radio – by catching the key words and identifying a main sentence.

Embark on a Journey Listen to an Oceanographer

- Listen to a TED conference talk by Sylvia Earle, a legendary ocean researcher and a devoted advocate for marine preservation.

[TED] My wish: Protecting our oceans / Sylvia Earle

https://www.ted.com/talks/sylvia_earle_s_ted_prize_wish_to_protect_our_oceans/

- While listening to the talk, answer the following questions:
  - o What were the rhetoric, metaphors, and quotes that impressed you?
  - o What statistical data did the speaker refer to to highlight the seriousness of marine pollution and depletion?
  - o What crises on marine environment have been brought into the attention in the talk? List as much as you can identify.
  - o What solution(s) does the speaker suggest to protect the marine environment?
- In pairs or groups, match and share your answers to the questions.

Crises on Marine Environment

Here are some of the types of marine pollution and depletion that are bearing harmful consequences to the marine environment.

Ocean Acidification

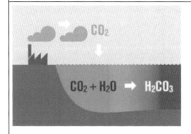

- **Definition:** As the levels of carbon dioxide (CO_2) increase in the atmosphere, the ocean continues to absorb more CO_2. Ocean acidification refers to this change in ocean chemistry, which results in dire consequences on the marine ecosystem.

- **Impact:** As carbonic acid (H_2CO_3) is formed when CO_2 dissolves into seawater, the concentration of carbonate ions (CO_3^{2-}) will decrease. Carbonate ions are critical ingredient for calcium carbonate ($CaCO_3$) structures, such as seashells and coral reefs. Therefore, it will be more difficult for calcifying marine organisms to build and maintain calcium carbonate structures.

- **Reference:** NOAA Ocean Acidification Program
  http://oceanacidification.noaa.gov/OurChangingOcean.aspx

Marine Debris

- **Definition:** Marine debris refers to manmade persistent solid waste that floats on or is suspended in the ocean. Anything that we use in our daily life can result in as marine debris if not disposed properly. Plastic marine debris is the most common type (80%), including microplastic that is invisible to naked eyes.

- **Impact:** Marine species often get tangled in marine debris and get injured or even die if they cannot untangle. Marine debris eaten by marine animals can also cause dire damage to their health. Toxic chemicals in marine debris will remain in fish and will also affect humans as we consume fish. Marine habitats like coral reefs can be destroyed by marine debris, depriving home for many marine creatures.

- **Reference:** NOAA Marine Debris Program https://marinedebris.noaa.gov/

Harmful Algal Blooms

- **Definition:** When colonies of algae grow out of control, oxygen inside natural waters decreases dramatically and some algae-produced toxins can spread. This phenomenon is called a harmful algal bloom (HAB), which most frequently occurs in the coastal area and can last from a few days to several months.
- **Impact:** When a HAB occurs, marine animals can suffer due to lack of oxygen and spread of toxins. After the bloom dies, the mocirobes that decomposes the algae use up even more oxygen and massive fish die-offs may occur. Eating fish or shellfish during the HAB can result in food poisoning in humans and other animals. It is also not safe to swim or play watersports during the bloom. When toxins are found in the place where drinking water is drawn, more careful provision on public water system is required.
- **References:** NOAA on HAB https://oceanservice.noaa.gov/hazards/hab/
  EPA on HAB https://www.epa.gov/nutrientpollution/harmful-algal-blooms

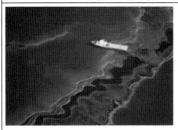

Oil and Chemical Spills

- **Definition:** An oil and chemical spill generally refers to the release of liquid petroleum hydrocarbon into the ocean or coastal waters. It may occur due to releases of crude oil (unrefined oil) from oil tankers, offshore platforms, and offshore drilling rigs and wells, as well as due to spills of refined petroleum due to marine accidents.
- **Impact:** The release of oil and chemicals can kill marine life, destroy their habitat, damage aquafarms, and contaminate critical resources in our food chain. Spills can play havoc with the coastal economy by forcing the closure of fisheries, shutting down tourism and businesses, and closing some marine navigation routes. These damages on environment and economy can last for decades.
- **Reference:** NOAA on spills https://oceanservice.noaa.gov/hazards/spills/

Overfishing

- **Definition:** Overfishing refers to overexploitation of fish stocks below acceptable levels. Based on scientifically studied population estimates and stock growth indexes, the acceptable amount of fishing is determined and regulated by the Fisheries agency in each country.
- **Impact:** Overfishing can result in marine resource depletion, and if it continues, it can lead to critical depensation where the fish population is no longer able to sustain itself. This may result in local extinction of certain fish species. Also, overfishing of upper predator species (e.g. sharks) may upset the entire marine ecosystem.
- **Reference:** NOAA Fisheries https://www.fisheries.noaa.gov/national/population-assessments/status-us-fisheries

Sailing Forward Campaign for Marine Environment

- In pairs or groups, choose one issue poses threat to the marine environment, and prepare a brief presentation on the issue. (1) Introduce the issue, (2) explain its cause and consequences to the marine environment, and (3) draw a conclusion (asking for change or action) with a catchphrase. Use <u>one or more</u> of the following techniques:
  - o Use rhetoric, metaphors, or quotes to convey a strong message.
  - o Illustrate the issue through vivid examples or statistics taken from articles, movies, or books to persuade the audience.
  - o Tell a personal story or anecdote related the issue to make your message more personal and appealing to the audience.
  - o Use visual aids to support your verbal delivery.
- After listening to the presentation, the audience responds to each presentation by writing comments and putting them on a comment board.
  - o Point out what went well, and what can be improved in the presentation.
  - o Share your personal thoughts and feelings.

Speaking Tackle 6 Connecting Sentences

Using shorter utterances/sentences is a good strategy when you aim to speak out your thoughts fluently in real time, and to avoid errors. However, in the end this may limit your repertoires of speech since it allows less variation in grammar and expressions. When you deliver a prepared speech, it would sound more stylish if you include a variety of sentence forms. Also, if you choose to combine or connect simple sentences into longer and more complex sentences, you can express your nuance and attitude much better by defining the relationships between two statements clearly.

Conjunction
• Simple words that connect two sentences to express simple logical relationships without having to change the nuances of original sentences (i.e. *and, but, nor, or, so, yet, for…*) e.g. I heard astronaut Joe Allen explain how he had to learn everything he could about his life support system and then do everything he could to take care of his life support system; and then he pointed to this [the earth] and he said, "Life support system." – From Sylvia Earle's speech *My wish: Protect our oceans* Q. Why do you think the speaker combined the two sentences and made them to a single long sentence?

Coordination

• Words or phrases that play somewhat overlapping roles with the simple conjunctions, but adds on more subtlety of meanings
  o *Consequently, therefore*: Something happened as a consequence or logical follow-up of the preceding event.
  o *Furthermore, in addition, moreover*: Similar to *and*, but extends the meaning of the preceding statement or event.
  o *Indeed, in fact*: Similar to *and*, but adds details to the preceding statement or event to emphasize the preceding statement or event.

Speaking Tackle 6 Connecting Sentences

o *However*: Similar to *but*, only for longer sentences.

o *Nevertheless*: Similar to *but*, but the meaning of previous statement or event has been emphasized (in terms of its significance or severity)

o *Then*: Something happened after the previous event.

Q. Combine the following two sentences with a connector that you think suits well. Compare your answer with a partner and discuss how the meaning or nuance has changed.

Sylvia seems to be a workaholic. She dedicated her whole life to navigating the marine life and environment.

Discourse connectors

• Words or phrases that are inserted at the beginning of a sentence to express its clear association with a previous utterance/sentence. Some of them can be used in other positions than the sentence initial (e.g. *consequently, therefore, however, in fact, nevertheless, then...*)

o Indicating the result: *therefore, consequently, in consequence, as a result, accordingly, hence, thus, for this reason, because of this ...*

o Indicating why: *because, since, as, insofar as ...*

o Adding the meaning: *moreover, in addition, additionally, furthermore, also, besides, what is more ...*

o Adding details: *in fact, as a matter of fact, indeed ...*

o Making a contrast: *however, on the other hand, in contrast, yet ...*

o Making a concession: *although, even though, despite (the fact that), in spite of (the fact that), regardless of (the fact that) ...*

o Expressing a condition: *if, in the event of, as long as, so long as, provided that, assuming that, given that...*

Dive into Vocabulary

Search or guess the meanings of vocabulary or phrases below before listening. While listening, make a better guess of the meanings of vocabulary or phrases.

- briny (adj.)
- out of my element / out of my comfort zone
- canary in a coal mine
- familiar turf
- sweetwater (n.)
- hatchery (n.)
- die-off (n.)
- acidic (adj.) / acidification (n.)
- curl up in ~
- fetal (adj.)
- seagrass (n.)
- a glimmer of hope
- photosynthesis (n.)
- buffer (n.)
- promising (adj.)
- a silver bullet
- kelp (n.)
- on the ground

Dive into Grammar

So far, the results look **promising,** but not necessarily a silver bullet.

In English, there are many adjectives ending in –ing and –ed such as **boring** and **bored.** If a person is **boring,** this means that he or she makes other people **bored.**

- Patrick always talks about the same things. He's really **boring.**
- Justin thinks politics is **interesting.** / Justin is **interested** in politics.
- The movie was **disappointing.** / We were **disappointed** with the movie.

Listen to the news on efforts to save oysters from marine acidification.
[NPR] Can seagrass save shellfish from climate change?
https://www.npr.org/sections/thesalt/2018/01/30/580999790/can-seaweed-save-shellfish-from-climate-change
For transcripts:
https://www.npr.org/templates/transcript/transcript.php?storyId=580999790

Guiding Questions

1. Why did Terry Sawyer attend climate change conferences? What issue did he address in the conference?

2. What was happening in the hatcheries from which Sawyer buys baby oysters? What is thought to be the main cause?

3. Why is the seawater becoming more acidic, according to the article?

4. What solution is Kristy Kroeker testing to protect baby oysters? How can seagrass make the seawater less acidic?

5. Why is seagrass not a silver bullet to seawater acidification?

Listening Lighthouse

6. What is the upside of using seagrass to prevent acidification? What can be improved?

Listening to Speaking

• Draw a diagram of causes, results, and solutions mentioned in the article.

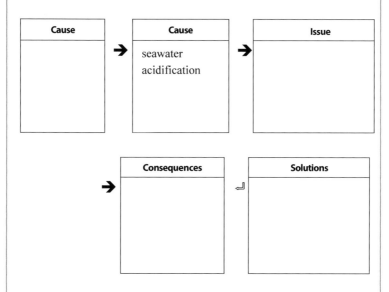

• [Pair or group] Referring to the diagram, summarize the news verbally in about 3-5 sentences. Use the sentence connectors suggested in **Speaking Tackle 6** (pp. 124-125) to give variation and indicate the logical relationships between the sentences.

Chapter 12. Saving the Future of the Sea

Chapter Forecast

- In this chapter, you will learn how to organize your speech into an effective opening, followed by a body, and a closing.
- You will practice how to share your opinion in a pair or small group, as well as in a whole class setting.
- You will learn practical tips to understand a short interview in a radio – by catching the key words and identifying a main sentence.

Embark on a Journey Ideas to Save the Sea

- In pairs or groups, come up with the names of movies that are setting in the oceans or seas.
- Pick three movies that you think are best associated with the oceans or seas.
- Search on the web the names of oceans or seas the movies set in.
- Identify on the map the geographic location each movie set in.
- Discuss the reasons why you chose the three movies and why you think the movies are best associated with the oceans or seas.

Ideas to Save the Sea

Here are some of the types of marine pollution and depletion that are bearing harmful consequences to the marine environment.

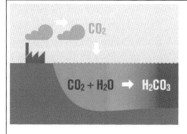

Ocean Acidification

- **Definition:** As the levels of carbon dioxide (CO_2) increase in the atmosphere, the ocean continues to absorb more CO_2. Ocean acidification refers to this change in ocean chemistry, which results in dire consequences on the marine ecosystem.
- **Impact:** As carbonic acid (H_2CO_3) is formed when CO_2 dissolves into seawater, the concentration of carbonate ions (CO_3^{2-}) will decrease. Carbonate ions are critical ingredient for calcium carbonate ($CaCO_3$) structures, such as seashells and coral reefs. Therefore, it will be more difficult for calcifying marine organisms to build and maintain calcium carbonate structures.
- **Reference:** NOAA Ocean Acidification Program http://oceanacidification.noaa.gov/OurChangingOcean.aspx

Marine Debris

- **Definition:** Marine debris refers to manmade persistent solid waste that floats on or is suspended in the ocean. Anything that we use in our daily life can result in as marine debris if not disposed properly. Plastic marine debris is the most common type (80%), including microplastic that is invisible to naked eyes.
- **Impact:** Marine species often get tangled in marine debris and get injured or even die if they cannot untangle. Marine debris eaten by marine animals can also cause dire damage to their health. Toxic chemicals in marine debris will remain in fish and will also affect humans as we consume fish. Marine habitats like coral reefs can be destroyed by marine debris, depriving home for many marine creatures.
- **Reference:** NOAA Marine Debris Program https://marinedebris.noaa.gov/

Harmful Algal Blooms

- **Definition:** When colonies of algae grow out of control, oxygen inside natural waters decreases dramatically and some algae-produced toxins can spread. This phenomenon is called a harmful algal bloom (HAB), which most frequently occurs in the coastal area and can last from a few days to several months.

- **Impact:** When a HAB occurs, marine animals can suffer due to lack of oxygen and spread of toxins. After the bloom dies, the mocirobes that decomposes the algae use up even more oxygen and massive fish die-offs may occur. Eating fish or shellfish during the HAB can result in food poisoning in humans and other animals. It is also not safe to swim or play watersports during the bloom. When toxins are found in the place where drinking water is drawn, more careful provision on public water system is required.

- **References:** NOAA on HAB https://oceanservice.noaa.gov/hazards/hab/
  EPA on HAB https://www.epa.gov/nutrientpollution/harmful-algal-blooms

Oil and Chemical Spills

- **Definition:** An oil and chemical spill generally refers to the release of liquid petroleum hydrocarbon into the ocean or coastal waters. It may occur due to releases of crude oil (unrefined oil) from oil tankers, offshore platforms, and offshore drilling rigs and wells, as well as due to spills of refined petroleum due to marine accidents.

- **Impact:** The release of oil and chemicals can kill marine life, destroy their habitat, damage aquafarms, and contaminate critical resources in our food chain. Spills can play havoc with the coastal economy by forcing the closure of fisheries, shutting down tourism and businesses, and closing some marine navigation routes. These damages on environment and economy can last for decades.

- **Reference:** NOAA on spills https://oceanservice.noaa.gov/hazards/spills/

Overfishing

- **Definition:** Overfishing refers to overexploitation of fish stocks below acceptable levels. Based on scientifically studied population estimates and stock growth indexes, the acceptable amount of fishing is determined and regulated by the Fisheries agency in each country.

- **Impact:** Overfishing can result in marine resource depletion, and if it continues, it can lead to critical depensation where the fish population is no longer able to sustain itself. This may result in local extinction of certain fish species. Also, overfishing of upper predator species (e.g. sharks) may upset the entire marine ecosystem.

- **Reference:** NOAA Fisheries https://www.fisheries.noaa.gov/national/ population-assessments/status-us-fisheries

---

Sailing Forward Turning Ideas to a Proposal

- [Whole Class] Find out rhyming words in English poems.
    - o Circle rhyming words in "I started Early –Took my Dog" and "Sea Fever".
    - o Are there any patterns in the places where rhyming words appear?

Writing Tackle 6 Writing a Proposal

You want to write a proposal for grant or funding, competitions, or social campaigns? That's great news! This means that you have a valuable idea for research or activism to benefit the community or to develop your passion. In fact, your vision of how to make something better can be improved through writing a proposal.

Your imagination and other's feedback are the two important ingredients for successful writing. Take a note of your ideas any time, and bring up your worthwhile ideas to the conversation if you need support. When your ideas become concrete, don't hesitate to draft it into a proposal!

Here are some golden rules and common elements of a good proposal:

Golden Rules

- **Consider your audience:** Think about the people who will read the proposal. If they are people from an agency or company, what are its mission, goals, and values? How is your proposal aligned with what the agency or company pursues? If they are the general public, what group of people is most likely to pay attention or participate in your campaign? How would you align what you want to do with what people care about in their life? Elaborate your plan by answering these questions, using the vocabulary that is familiar to them, laying the background and frame that they are seeking for.

- **Meet the expectations:** Pay attention to all the requirements of grant, a competition, or a platform that you are submitting your proposal. Your proposal should adhere exactly to these requirements. Study the samples of successful proposals that have received the funding or approval from where you are applying.

- **Be logical, consistent, and credible:** Make sure your writing is clear and logical in terms of its format and content. Divide your proposal into predictable sections and label with clear headings. Present that yourself as capable, knowledgeable, and forward thinking. Reference your past accomplishments that verify your consistent interest and ability to succeed in this project.

Writing Tackle 6 **Writing a Proposal**

Common Elements

- **Short overview:** You present the most important elements of your project in as few words as possible. Condense your idea to one short paragraph containing (1) the purpose or goal of your project, (2) the need or problem your project addresses, (3) expected outcomes, (4) why your project matters to the community.

- **Addressing a need or problem:** In order to establish the value of your project, you need to clarify what need or problem your project responds to. Make sure that you establish the context of this problem (i.e. the background), and describe what group of people is affected by this problem. Include data if necessary. If you are writing an academic proposal, be sure to include a short literature review clarifying that you have extensive understanding on the topic, field, and the scholarly context of your project.

- **Description of your project:** Describe your project by answering the following questions.
  - o What are the goals of your project?
  - o What will your project's outcomes be?
  - o How are you going to achieve those outcomes? What are your methods?
  - o How will you measure or recognize the achievements? What are the milestones?
  - o What will be the timeline for your project?

- **Budget plan:** If you are asking for monetary support, you need to clarify and justify how much amount of budget is required for what reason. Budgets are often formatted in tables and figures with a justification statement explaining why the cost is valid, reasonable, and important for your project.

Dive into Vocabulary

Search or guess the meanings of vocabulary or phrases below before listening.
While listening, make a better guess of the meanings of vocabulary or phrases.

- bedrock (n.)
- sprawl map
- homogenize (v.)
- plummet (v.)
- meld (v.)
- object in the field
- devoid of context
- blatant (adj.)
- albeit
- manifesto
- "oyster-tecture" oyster + architecture
- harness (v.)
- eelgrass (n.)
- inundation (n.)
- upland (n.)
- intuit
- dredge (v.)
- sewage (n.)
- exacerbate (v.)
- a matrix of salt marshes and beaches
- attenuation
- detritus
- ubiquitous
- the short end of the deal
- agglomerate (v.)
- spat (n.)
- "the answers won't land down from the Moon."
- bake sale
- amphibious (adj.)
- Tevas (n.)
- hybridize (v.)
- "flupsy" an acronym for floating upwelling system
- churn (v.)
- sink your teeth into ~

Dive into Grammar

James: I probably made that movie because I believed I could actually dive to the Titanic. And **if I could have** actually **dived** to the Titanic without making the movie, I probably **would have done** that.

If I had known you were in the hospital, **I would have gone** to see you.

If the weather hadn't been so bad, we **might have gone out** to eat at a French restaurant.

As shown in the above sentences, we use **if + had (could have) + past perfect** followed by **would/could/might + have + past perfect** to talk about the past wish that did not come true ("counterfactual conditional").

Listening Lighthouse

Listen to the following proposal on reviving rivers and seaport with oyster farming.
[TED] Reviving New York's Rivers-With Oysters! / Kate Orff
https://www.ted.com/talks/kate_orff_oysters_as_architecture/up-next

Guiding Questions

1. How would you define the speaker's research interest? What theoretical framework and concepts does she bring in to her project?

2. What relationships does Kate observe from the graph that maps changes in urban population, the sea level, temperature, and the number of species? Why do you think she used this graph in her presentation?

3. According to the speaker, what kind of paradigm shift is occurring in the field of design and architecture?

4. Why is Kate attracted to oysters? What is "oyster-tecture"?

5. What problems are the Gowanus Canal and the Governor's Island facing?

6. Why does Kate pay attention to the history of New York to solve the current problems?

7. What are the three core issues that the project addresses? How can oyster be a solution to these issues?
   a)
   b)
   c)

8. How does the oyster reef system work? What is the material and method were used to build the reef system?

9. What are the extra perks of the oyster reef system?

10. Why are the benefits of "flupsy" in growing baby oysters?

Personal Take

• Is Kate's proposal following all or most of the golden rules and containing the common elements of proposal? Explain how.

• What do you think are the strengths of her proposal as a solution to cope with river/harbor contamination?

• What questions or criticism do you have regarding her proposal?

• What did you like about her presentation? What skills would you like to incorporate into your own presentation?

Appendix

The following are cited reading materials for relevant chapters in the coursebook.

Chapter 2. Maritime Weather Forecasting

https://www.maritimeinjurycenter.com/accidents-and-injuries/weather-forecasting/

Maritime activities are always risky, but there are many things that mariners and seamen can do to reduce the risks. Weather is one of several factors that cause maritime work and recreation to be risky and dangerous, but forecasting the weather can help prevent accidents that lead to shipping and cargo losses, injuries, and even fatalities.

Weather can be difficult to predict, especially on waterways, but good forecasting can help ships and their crews navigate and make decisions that reduce risks. Bad weather can cause ships and boats to capsize, to run aground, or to collide with other ships or objects. Knowing what kind of weather is coming is extremely important in making maritime activities safer.

Weather at Sea

Weather at sea is not the same as weather over land. The main driving forces are winds, including the trade winds, which blow to the west in the tropical oceans, and the westerlies, which blow to the east in the mid-latitude regions. Winds create surface ocean currents by dragging across the water. In the northern hemisphere, these currents move in clockwise rotations while in the southern hemisphere, they move in counterclockwise rotations.

There are also smaller currents that move along the edges of the major currents, called gyres. The smaller, boundary currents are numerous and include the Gulf Stream, which moves from the Gulf of Mexico, along the eastern coast of the U.S. and Canada, and across the ocean to the British Isles. These currents generate and influence much of the maritime weather that we see across the world's oceans.

Weather generates waves and swells, which have a big impact on vessels. Winds produce waves in the oceans, and the size of the waves depends on the strength and duration of winds and how far the winds blow without interruption. Swells are groups of large waves that outrun the wind or storm that generated them. Ships at sea may also face rogue waves, unusually large waves among smaller waves. These can cause a lot of damage.

Waves and winds occurring together during storms are particularly dangerous and include hurricanes, also called typhoons and cyclones. These are very large and damaging storms. They are high-speed winds rotating around a calm center, called an eye. Predicting the formation, strength, duration, and path of a hurricane is an important part of maritime forecasting.

Accidents That Can Be Caused by Weather

Maritime weather can be unpredictable, and this is why forecasting it is so important. Forecasting isn't perfect, but it does give navigators and other crew the ability to make better decisions about routes. The main types of weather that can cause maritime accidents are high winds, storms, and waves or swells. Any of these can cause ships to list heavily, which in turn can cause on-board accidents. Shifting cargo and equipment, falls, and overboard accidents can all result from rough weather and listing ships.

Ships can also get blown off course by severe weather, which can lead to serious accidents. These include running aground in shallow waters or on reefs, which can damage ships, throw crew members overboard, and even cause a ship to sink.

Weather can even cause a ship to run into another ship or an object like a bridge, which can cause similar accidents.

Weather Forecasting Methods

Forecasting can be done in multiple ways. Satellites are important for tracking weather across oceans and other bodies of water. Meteorological satellites are dedicated to tracking weather and include those that orbit at the poles of the earth, stationary satellites that monitor just one part of Earth's surface, and satellites that orbit the entire planet. Satellites can gather information about clouds, temperature of the air and water, currents, dust storms, ice coverage, and more.

Maritime weather is also monitored by weather buoys and weather ships. A moored buoy is a stationary device that can be tethered to one part of the ocean to collect weather information. There are also drifting buoys that track weather as they move across oceans. There are currently more than 1,000 drifting weather buoys across the world, helping to forecast marine weather.

Information taken from these weather stations and satellite is used by meteorologists and computer software to model currents and winds, to track temperatures and storms, and to predict what weather will happen next, where it will happen, and how it may impact ships and other vessels on the oceans.

Weather Forecasting Responsibilities

There are various official organizations around the world that are responsible for tracking and predicting maritime weather and sharing that information with the public and with commercial maritime operations. In the U.S. the National Weather Service of the National Oceanic and Atmospheric Administration tracks and predicts maritime weather, providing maps, forecasts, hazards, warnings, weather and storm models, and many other types of information that can be used by anyone heading out on the water.

Around the world, many countries have their own weather tracking systems and agencies. Internationally, the World Meteorological Organization provides guidelines for how these agencies operate and provide information in international waters.

The Importance of Using Marine Weather Forecasting

The information provided by marine weather forecasting

agencies is important for preventing accidents by avoid storms and other weather-related hazards. The consequences of not using that information, of ignoring it, or of misusing or misjudging the information can be serious. One tragic example is the disastrous accident of the El Faro cargo ship.

The El Faro was lost in Caribbean waters on October 1, 2015. A month later the ship was found, sunk, and all 33 members of the crew died. The ship had sailed right into Hurricane Joaquin on its way from Florida to Puerto Rico. The subsequent investigation found that the captain, an experienced seaman, had the forecasting information about the storm but erred when he decided to keep the ship's course and go right through the hurricane. Even with the best predictive information, crew members can make flawed decisions about weather that lead to disastrous results.

Maritime weather forecasting is an important tool for anyone in the maritime industry, from cargo ship captains to crew on smaller fishing vessels. Weather can be highly unpredictable, but good forecasting can help crew make better choices and avoid the kinds of disasters that can lead to °tragic accidents, injuries, lost cargo, ship damage, and lost lives.

Chapter 5. The World of Marine Bio-Resources

[NPR] Countries Pledge To Recover Dwindling Pacific Bluefin Tuna Population

https://www.npr.org/sections/thesalt/2017/09/01/547903557/countries-pledge-to-recover-dwindling-pacific-bluefin-tuna-population

September 1, 20173:50 PM ET
CLARE LESCHIN-HOAR

Tuna are arranged prior to the first auction of the year at Tsukiji Fish Market in Tokyo, Japan. The new agreement to protect Pacific bluefin tuna is aimed at putting the species on a path to recovery by setting sliding catch limits.
The Asahi Shimbun/Getty Images

When it comes to bluefin tuna, it's not often we have good news to share, but spin the globe today, and there's cause for celebration in both the Pacific and Atlantic. In a joint meeting Friday in Busan, South Korea, the two groups that manage Pacific bluefin tuna reached a historic long-term agreement that would put the species on the path to recovery. The Western and Central Pacific Fisheries Commission and the Inter-American Tropical Tuna Commission agreed to take steps to rebuild the population to 20 percent of historic levels by 2034—a sevenfold increase from current levels.

Stocks of Pacific bluefin have fallen to 2.6 percent of their historic size, with countries like Mexico, Japan, Korea and the U.S. exceeding fishing quotas within the last two years. This is a population in dire need of the protection that finally arrived Friday.

The groups agreed to establish sliding catch limits to reach that goal, based on how well the stocks recover in coming years, and have agreed to a harvest strategy timeline that includes stakeholder meetings over the next two years. The management groups have also committed to finding ways to prevent illegally caught bluefin tuna from reaching markets.

"The really big, exciting thing is they have all agreed to a 20 percent target for recovery. It's the level at which you can say this population really has a chance," says Amanda Nickson, director of Global Tuna Conservation at Pew Charitable Trusts.

"This is a resilient population," says Nickson. In other words, if the fish are allowed to survive and reproduce, the population is likely to bounce back. Also important, she adds, is that the rebuilding target will still allow for some fishing activity. That's key to maintaining the tuna fleet as stocks replenish.

The news comes on the heels of the National Marine Fisheries Service's closure this week of the U.S. commercial Pacific bluefin fishery for the remaining four months of the year after fishermen exceeded the 2017 quota of 425 metric tons.

Environmental groups were disappointed last month when the U.S. federal government denied a petition to list Pacific bluefin tuna as an endangered species.

Chris Yates, assistant regional administrator for NOAA Fisheries West Coast Region, says there's a different bar when evaluating for endangered species protection. "We need to determine that the species is likely to become extinct or is likely to become endangered of extinction in the foreseeable future," he says.

There are currently 1.6 million Pacific bluefin in the Pacific, and of those, 145,000 are reproducing adults. "So while the numbers of bluefin tuna are much less than desirable, there are still a lot out there," says Yates.

Despite the disappointment of the petition's denial, Friday's agreement is likely to help populations rebound. And the good news doesn't stop there.

This spring, rumors began to swirl among the scientific and environmental communities that Atlantic bluefin tuna ─ an iconic species, whose declining population levels have prompted hand-wringing as far back as 1991 — may finally have achieved full recovery.

But like many juicy rumors, it was only partially true.

Scientists responsible for gathering data and making recommendations to the International Commission for the Conservation of Atlantic Tunas, the fishery management body for Atlantic bluefin tuna, say preliminary numbers show stocks are indeed rebounding.

"Some models have the stock skyrocketing to higher levels than we saw in the 1950s. Other models use more information and account for uncertainty in the data," says Clay Porch, the bluefin tuna coordinator for the Standing Committee for Research and Statistics for ICCAT and director of NOAA's Sustainable Fisheries Division.

"This year's [assessment] was different because of the sheer amount of new information we were trying to incorporate," Porch says.

ICCAT and the scientific community as a whole expended a lot of resources mining historical data and collecting new data. They performed tagging studies and expanded biological sampling of the fish to help determine age, genetics and where the fish were born.

"It was a complicated affair," he says.

Although they share an ocean, Atlantic bluefin tuna are actually counted as two distinct stocks. The significantly larger stock comes from the Eastern Atlantic and Mediterranean. The Western Atlantic stock, which swim off American shores and spawn in the Gulf of Mexico, is the smaller of the two. The latest assessment suggests both stocks are improving, with the greatest growth coming from tuna in the Eastern Atlantic.

"After decades of mismanagement and illegal fishing ... the good news is the managers have followed the scientific advice and it shows that science-based management of Atlantic bluefin is working," says Rachel Hopkins, senior officer at The Pew Charitable Trusts' Global Tuna Conservation program.

But Hopkins cautions that there's reason to believe that the stock closer to home isn't recovering as robustly. There is concern that what appears to be population growth in the Western Atlantic bluefin could be inflated because Eastern bluefin have been migrating over and mixing with the Western stock.

"Western [stock is] growing, but there is concern that growth may not be growth at all," says Hopkins. "But Eastern Atlantic bluefin are certainly cause for celebration."

And it looks like that good news could someday be mirrored in the Pacific, if Friday's agreement and goals are reached.

Clare Leschin-Hoar is a journalist based in San Diego who covers food policy and sustainability issues.

Chapter 7. Marine Transportation

[NYT] South Korea Raises Ferry That Sank in 2014 Disaster

https://www.nytimes.com/2017/03/22/world/asia/south-korea-ferry-sewol.html

South Korea Raises Ferry That Sank in 2014 Disaster
By CHOE SANG-HUN MARCH 22, 2017

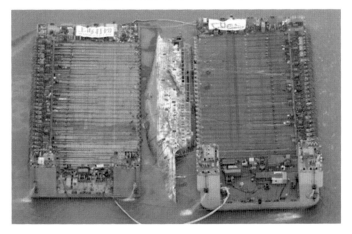

Workers in South Korea on Thursday raised the ferry Sewol, which capsized and sank in April 2014. More than 300 people died, many of them students.

SEOUL, South Korea — A South Korean ferry that sank nearly three years ago, killing more than 300 people — most of them teenagers on a school trip — was raised to the surface on Thursday. It was an emotional moment for families who are still looking for their missing children and a step toward closing one of the most traumatic episodes in South Korea's history.

The ferry, the 6,825-ton Sewol, capsized and sank off the southwestern tip of South Korea on April 16, 2014. The accident was the country's worst catastrophe in decades, and it contributed to the recent ouster of President Park Geun-hye. The ship went under while teenagers trapped inside sent text messages asking for help that never came or saying goodbye to their families.

A months-long underwater search of the ship ended after 295 bodies were recovered. Nine people who were on board remain missing, including four students and two teachers from Danwon High School in Ansan, south of Seoul, the South Korean capital. Of the 324 students from the school on board for a field trip, 250 drowned.

Salvage operations on Thursday. Divers spent months placing 33 lifting beams underneath the ferry and tying cables to both ends of them. Two salvage barges began pulling up the cables on Wednesday, raising the ship inch by inch.

Bereaved families have demanded that the ship be salvaged, hoping that the bodies of the missing would be found inside. They also hoped that the wreckage would reveal more clues to what caused the ship to sink. Government investigators have blamed overloading, the ship's structural imbalance and poor decisions by the crew for the disaster.

In 2015, the government announced plans to raise the ship, contracting a consortium of Chinese and South Korean salvage crews for the $76 million operation. Their work has been painstakingly slow because of strong currents, frequent periods of bad weather, poor underwater visibility and the complicated engineering maneuvers needed to raise the ship, which was lying on its side about 145 feet below the surface.

Divers spent months placing 33 lifting beams underneath the ferry and tying cables to both ends of them. After days of testing, two salvage barges began pulling up the cables on Wednesday, raising the ship inch by inch.

By Thursday morning, the ferry's mud-covered, rusting hull

broke through the surface, and workers began fastening the ferry to the barges.

Ships involved in the salvage operation. Work has been painstakingly slow because of bad weather and the complicated engineering maneuvers needed to raise the ship, which was lying about 145 feet below the surface.

Credit Ed Jones/Agence France-Presse — Getty Images

Family members of the victims watched the operation overnight from a government ship.

In the next couple of weeks, the ferry will be transferred to a semi-submersible

vessel, which will lift it out of the water completely and carry it to Mokpo, a port 55 miles away. There, officials will conduct a thorough search.

The investigation of the sinking has exposed numerous loopholes in safety standards in South Korea.

The Sewol's operator, Chonghaejin Marine, routinely overloaded the ship with poorly secured cargo, including on the ferry's final voyage. Inspectors colluded in the practice by giving the Sewol and other ships just a cursory check from the pier, or none at all. When the Sewol capsized, its crew members were among the first to flee, after repeatedly telling passengers to stay in their cabins.

The first Coast Guard boat that arrived at the scene did little more than pick up the fleeing crew members, while passengers trapped inside the ferry banged on the windows as the ship slowly disappeared beneath the waves.

The captain of the ferry, Lee Jun-seok, was sentenced to life in prison after being convicted of murder through willful negligence. Fourteen other crew members received prison sentences of 18 months to 12 years. Dozens of ferry company officials, safety inspectors and Coast Guard officials have also been jailed or convicted on various criminal charges related to the sinking.

Relatives of victims of the Sewol ferry disaster watched the salvage effort from the southern island of Donggeochado on Wednesday. Bereaved families have demanded that the ship be salvaged, hoping to recover the bodies of the missing.

Credit Ed Jones/Agence France-Presse — Getty Images

Many South Koreans remain outraged by the disaster. Some of the bereaved family members and sympathetic activists have camped out in Seoul and kept watch on the salvage operation from islands near the site, calling for a more thorough investigation into the government's response.

When huge crowds of people rallied in central Seoul in recent months to demand that Ms. Park be removed, the government's botched rescue operation was a central grievance voiced against the president. When lawmakers in the National Assembly voted to impeach her on Dec. 9, they accused her of negligence in the handling of the disaster.

When the Constitutional Court formally removed Ms. Park from office on March 10, it said she had stayed in her residence, not in her office, for seven hours after she first heard of the sinking. But the court said her actions in that case were not grounds to oust her. Instead, the court voted to remove Ms. Park based on other charges, including corruption and abuse of power.

Despite the court's ruling, the disaster was the biggest blot on Ms. Park's record as president. Many South Koreans saw her failure to take charge of the emergency as emblematic of what they considered her aloofness as leader.

A version of this article appears in print on March 23, 2017, on Page A4 of the New York edition with the headline: South Korea Raises Ferry That Capsized in 2014.

Chapter 8. Maritime History

[The Guardian] Maritime museum finds time for celebration of Harrison's sea clock

https://www.theguardian.com/culture/2014/jul/09/ships-clocks-star s-longitude-act-maritime-museum-harrison-anniversary

Maritime museum finds time for celebration of Harrison's sea clocks

New exhibition marks 300th anniversary of the passing of the Longitude Act, and the clock making genius who made it happen

Maev Kennedy

Wed 9 Jul 2014 10.13 BST

First published on Wed 9 Jul 2014 10. 13 BST

There is a tormented man scribbling on the wall of Bedlam, in the background of Hogarth's final print of the famous 1735 Rake's Progress series, on show in a major new exhibition at the Maritime Museum in Greenwich. He has already drawn a globe striped with lines of latitude and – the £20,000 question torturing many of the best minds of scientists, mathematicians, naval officers and astronomers of the day – longitude. The poor man is covering the walls of the mental hospital with calculations, literally driven mad by the problem of longitude.

Beside it there is a loaned pirate copy of the print, made within a year of the publication of the bestselling series, the first time the two have ever been exhibited together. It was made by a hack draftsman who was sent to get a sneaky look at the originals and then draw as much as he could remember. He got most of the details but the debate about it has already moved on: the unfortunate is now agonising about clockwork mechanisms, and has written "the clock does strike by algebra".

"Both prints show that the longitude debate is perfectly familiar to both the draftsman, and the members of the public, who will know without any further explanation that the attempt to solve longitude is a huge joke, the problem that will never be solved," curator Richard Dunn said.

John Harrison's perfectly accurate clocks, which became the standard issue marine chronometer, essentially solved the problem. But none of this is ancient history, made obsolete by modern technology, Dunn insists: the skills so painfully won of using time and the stars to work out position at sea will be needed again.

"Already the navy is teaching more traditional navigation. Some time in the next 30 years there is going to be a catastrophic failure of GPS, either from the cascade effect, as in the film Gravity, or some dire world event which it is not pleasant to contemplate. And then we will be back to sea watches, sextants, and the stars."

It was no laughing matter for thousands of sailors shipwrecked because attempts to establish where they were in the ocean were hundreds of miles out. In a storm in 1707, when an entire British fleet was driven onto the rocks at Scilly believing they were safely out at sea, more than 1,400 sailors drowned.

The exhibition marks the 300th anniversary of the Longitude Act, passed in 1714, which established the Longitude Board and offered a vast £20,000 prize to anyone who could solve the problem of measuring longitude at sea. It includes the actual act of parliament, passed in the last weeks before the death of Queen Anne, on display for the first time.

The story of John Harrison, the carpenter and self-taught genius clockmaker who invented a series of ever more accurate clocks and then a cabbage-sized watch that solved the problem, but never got the full prize from the board, inspired Dava Sobel's bestselling book and film, Longitude.

All of the Harrison clocks, brought back to the museum from their home in the Observatory for the first time in decades, are ticking away beautifully in the exhibition. Just seven staff members, including Dunn and art curator Katy Barrett, are trusted with the task of winding them first thing each morning.

But as Dunn points out, the story began long before Harrison:

a sea clock was tested as early as the 1660s. "Many of the earlier solutions were highly ingenious, and worked very well – on dry land."

The exhibition brings together paintings, books, scientific instruments, letters from luminaries including Isaac Newton, and even the 18th-century astronomer royal Nevil Maskelyne's extraordinary padded silk romper suit for long, cold nights watching the stars. It continues for almost a century after Harrison's death, as research continued, and work on making instruments reliable and cheap enough to supply to every ship.

As well as the Harrison watch taken by Captain Cook, which he called "my trusty friend", the display includes a later version of the Harrison watch, issued to HMS Bounty. After the mutiny, when Fletcher Christian cast Captain Bligh adrift in the Bounty's longboat, the mutineers refused to give him the watch, making his surviving the 3,600 mile journey, in an open boat with his remaining loyal crew members, even more extraordinary. The watch went to Pitcairn, where it was eventually bought by a traveler and made its way back to England.

Ships, clocks and the stars: the quest for Longitude is at the National Maritime Museum, Greenwich, until 4 January 2014

Chapter 10. Tastes of the Sea

[FT] The sea women of Jeju

https://www.ft.com/content/e1ec5434-50f8-11e5-b029-b9d50a74fd14

The sea women of Jeju

For centuries, female divers on a South Korean island have made their living by harvesting seaweed. The women, some in their eighties, talk about a tradition that could soon be consigned to the past.

A group of sea women preparing to plunge to the ocean depths
Simon Mundy SEPTEMBER 5, 2015 5

Each of the elderly women utters a distinctive cry as they surface around me from the bitterly cold East China Sea, clutching fistfuls of seaweed. From my left comes a sound like the bleating of a goat; ahead, a determined groan of endurance. All of them are whistling too, an ancient technique to expel carbon dioxide from the lungs. Occasionally, the wetsuit-clad grandmothers exchange a few words after depositing their seaweed in sacks tied to orange buoys beside them. But none of them rests for more than a minute before plunging to the seabed once more — a rhythm they maintain for five hours.

These are the haenyeo (sea women) of South Korea's Jeju island, who have dived in search of seaweed and shellfish since at least the 17th century. Their work is one of the country's most celebrated traditions but one that many islanders fear could soon be consigned to the past.

Traditionally a job handed down from mother to daughter, haenyeo life has been shunned in recent decades by nearly all the girls born in Jeju's seaside villages, who have tended to favour more comfortable lives in the island's two cities or on the mainland. From more than 14,000 in the 1970s, the number of haenyeo has dwindled to fewer than 4,500 today.

The vast majority are aged over 50, with the oldest in their nineties. But, despite their age, they continue to perform feats beyond most women in their twenties — diving to depths of up to 20m, holding their breath for as long as two minutes at a time.

"These could be the last of the haenyeo," says Kim Hong-chul, who manages a diving association in the village of Jongdal-ri. "The haenyeo you see today had no education, no choice but to do that job. But now the young women want to do different things. It's a real problem for our community."

With the women at sea, the waterfront is deserted except for their elderly husbands, with cushions strapped to their backsides, who crouch as they sort their wives' catch of seaweed from the previous day.

Behind us, an old lady drives past on a small truck loaded with seaweed. "There goes Kwon Young-ae," Kim says. "She's finished diving a bit earlier than the others today because of her age — she's 85. Her older sister still dives too."

Half an hour later a fishing boat drifts into view, bearing two dozen women with more than a tonne of seaweed. As the husbands move in to greet them and deal with the catch, the women disembark, most of them trudging swiftly past their menfolk to a nearby changing room.

Ra Wal-soo, 89, donning her wetsuit as she gets ready to dive

A cohort of elderly freediving fisherwomen would stand out anywhere but especially so in South Korea, where fewer women work than in almost any other advanced economy, and where destitution among old people has become a national crisis. "Normally in South Korea the men take charge of the women but not in Jeju," says Kang Kwon-yong, curator of the nearby Haenyeo Museum. "These women have their own jobs, they earn their own money, they're the ones who resolve problems in the family. Most Koreans are still quite old-fashioned but these old ladies are the ones living in the 21st century."

A haenyeo carrying her haul and equipment on her back at
Aewol—eup on Jeju

The next morning I find about 30 haenyeo sheltering in the
shade of a bush at a roadside near Jongdal-ri and joshing among
themselves. Amid the banter, Yoo Ok-yeon, 62, sounds a darker
note as she considers the risks of putting elderly bodies through
such strenuous exercise and severe pressure changes. "We never
know in advance if we're going to die or not," she tells me. "So
many have died from heart attacks. The last one from our lot was
a couple of years ago. She didn't recognise that her blood oxygen
was getting too low." Yoo's fears are justified — an annual
average of nine haenyeo have died in the water over the past four
years.

After a brief pep talk from Kim, the haenyeo make their way
down to the sea, stepping with ease over sharp volcanic rocks
before dividing into two groups. I float among them as they
pursue a seemingly interminable cycle, swimming between seaweed

bag and sea floor. After five hours, the women stagger from the sea under bulging sacks of still-saturated seaweed, each weighing as much as 30kg. Oh Byeong-soon, a grandmother-of-six, is among the last to emerge — at 77 still one of the hardest workers in the village after more than half a century in a job she began aged 20.

"If I weren't diving, I'd just be growing potatoes," she says. "I dived right through pregnancy, up to the ninth month." This was normal practice, according to historians of Jeju, who record cases of haenyeo giving birth on boats during a day's diving, and even strapping their young children to the mast while they worked.

> **"**
>
> **Jeju men just leave their women to do all the work**

Historical records suggest diving was once a job for Jeju men but this changed in the 17th century, when the Korean king conscripted huge numbers of them into his army while still requiring large amounts of abalone to be sent to him as tribute. Fearful of recriminations, Jeju's women had no option but to take to the sea. The haenyeo have become emblematic of a distinctive culture of which islanders are fiercely proud — and which is acknowledged by mainlanders, who commonly complain that the strong Jeju dialect is virtually another language. The complex relationship between the two reached a horrific low point between 1948 and 1954, when Seoul's ruthless response to a leftwing rebellion on Jeju wiped out about a tenth of the island's population.

"That was a really tough time," recalls 80-year-old haenyeo Ahn Yong-seon, whom I find one day in the northern village of Iho where she is repairing her netted seaweed sack. Her husband was crippled in the violence, meaning she has had to support her family for her entire adult life. Soon, her work completed, she treads gingerly to her mobility scooter and slowly drives away.

Later I wade into the nearby sea, where other haenyeo are at work. One of them catches my eye and grins, brandishing a handful of seaweed. I ask her name. "Dunno, I'm 83," she replies with an impish smirk.

South Korea's elderly haenyeo divers Play video

Over the centuries, unique traditions have emerged among the divers, including songs that live on as haunting testaments to the hardships of their work. "One thing that can't be done is haenyeo work," one song goes. "As I enter the sea, the afterlife comes and goes...I eat wind instead of rice...take the waves as my home."

Still alive, too, is their unique form of Korean shamanism. Every February, haenyeo across Jeju hold a ceremony in honour of Yeongdeung Halmang, the goddess of the winds, sending straw boats out to sea to accompany her as she departs the island for another year. "They really believe in those gods — they believe the gods help them hold their breath," says Chua Hye-kyoung, who studies the haenyeo at the Jeju Development Institute. "They pray to be kept safe."

A haenyeo diving at Morado Island just off the coast of Jeju.

But in other ways the haenyeo life has changed with the times, I hear from Park Bong-sook, whom I meet near a luxury resort on

Jeju's east coast. As we talk, some attendees of an international conference wander down to photograph themselves at the adjacent lighthouse, barely glancing at Park and four other haenyeo drying their seaweed in the sun.

Born in 1945, Park started working as a haenyeo at 15 and spent a few years diving off the mainland's southern regions before returning at 23 to marry. "It would have been nice to marry a man from the mainland," she laughs. "Jeju men just leave their women to do all the work."

Kwon Young-ae finished diving a bit earlier than the others today because of her age — she's 85.

The biggest change, she says, came in the 1970s, when the government began subsidising wetsuits for the women, who had previously dived in loose cotton clothing, even in winter. "It was really hard, really freezing," she recounts, her cheerful demeanour suddenly absent as she mimes the suffering. "We just did it, because we were young. But it was hard to work for more than one or two hours at a time."

The wetsuits were a major advance that have enabled the haenyeo to boost their earnings by spending longer in the water, and to continue diving well into old age, says Kang at the Haenyeo Museum.

A diver jumps from a fishing boat off Jeju as other aenyeo lutch the orange buoys to which they attach their eaweed sacks

The most productive haenyeo earn up to Won30m ($25,000) a year, Kang says, though the local government estimates that most make less than half that from their diving. The women typically work intermittently in spring and winter — observing seasonal prohibitions to preserve stocks — and top up their income with second jobs, such as farming.

Their financial independence is remarkable in a country where elderly poverty is a huge problem. Forty-nine per cent of South Koreans over 65 live on less than half the median income — the highest proportion in the international Organisation for Economic Cooperation and Development (OECD), a group of advanced economies. That has contributed to a nearly fivefold increase in the elderly suicide rate since 1990 to a level that is by far the highest of any developed country.

Divers climbing over volcanic rock before entering the waters.

Such penury and despair is not shared by Koh Choon-san, who steadies herself against a baby's pushchair loaded with diving equipment as she watches her three daughters emerge from the sea on to the tiny island of Biyang. At 86, Koh is in her 70th year as a haenyeo, though she has now cut back to no more than 10 days a month in the water, and today is leaving the work to her daughters, whose ages range from 52 to 60.

89—year—old Ra Wal—soo comes up for air

Back at home, the sisters weigh their catch, the eldest reading out the weight of each bulging sack with a celebratory tone. In all, they have collected 110kg of seaweed in two hours, which they will sell for about Won1,000 ($1) per kilogramme. "I'll do it till I die," Koh says. But she is pessimistic about the future. "We don't have young women learning to do this," she says. "In about 30 years, our culture will be gone."

Yet just as the flexible nature of the work has enabled Koh to support herself into her ninth decade, it could also be the key to attracting a new generation of haenyeo.

A haenyeo taking off her wetsuit after a dive

In her home village on Jeju's south coast I meet Chae Ji-ae, 31, one of only a handful of haenyeo from her generation. Chae initially decided to steer clear of the job, working as a hairdresser in Seoul for a decade. Like many South Korean women, however, she struggled to balance her long working hours with the demands of motherhood. Having grown up watching her mother and grandmother work the ocean floor, the decision to return home and continue the family trade became obvious, though it meant moving away from her husband, who still works on the mainland. "Now I can have free time with my kids, work to the sound of the waves, enjoy the clean breeze," she says. "There might not be many of us in the future but I don't think we'll disappear completely.

Simon Mundy is the FT's Seoul correspondent. *Additional*

reporting by Shin Ha-young and Kang Buseong

The exhibition, HaeNyeo: Women of the Sea, by Hyung S. Kim was exhibited at The Korean Cultural Service New York and will tour internationally.

Photographs: Daun Kim

Slideshow photographs: Hyung S. Kim/Courtesy of Korean Cultural Service New York

Bibliography

Garrison, Tom. (2007). *Oceanography: An Invitation to Marine Science* (6th ed.).

Belmont, CA: Brooks/Cole Cengage Learning.

Hong, Ok Sook, Jhang, Se-Eun, Lee, Gunsoo, Noh, Jongjin, Parent, Kevin, & Ryoo, Mi-Lim. (2017). *Ocean Topics: Reading.* Busan, Korea: Hangil Publisher.

Hong, Ok Sook, Ryoo, Mi-Lim, Dawber, John, Dumas, Hilary, Kennedy, Allison, & Pepperdine, Wendell. (2017). *Ocean Topics: Advancing English Skills.* Seoul, Korea: Kyung Moon Sa Publisher.

Websites:

https://www.maritimeinjurycenter.com/accidents-and-injuries/weather-forecasting/

[NPR] Countries Pledge To Recover Dwindling Pacific Bluefin Tuna Population

https://www.npr.org/sections/thesalt/2017/09/01/547903557/countries-pledge-to-recover-dwindling-pacific-bluefin-tuna-population

[NYT] South Korea Raises Ferry That Sank in 2014 Disaster

https://www.nytimes.com/2017/03/22/world/asia/south-korea-ferry-sewol.html

[The Guardian] Maritime museum finds time for celebration of Harrison's sea clock

https://www.theguardian.com/culture/2014/jul/09/ships-clocks-stars-longitude-act-maritime-museum-harrison-anniversary

[FT] The sea women of Jeju

https://www.ft.com/content/e1ec5434-50f8-11e5-b029-b9d50a74fd14

BBC: www.bbc.com

NPR: www.npr.org

Mae-Ran Park ──────────────────────────────────

Dr. Mae-Ran Park is a professor of English Language and Literature Department at Pukyong National University, Korea. She obtained her Master's degree in Teaching of English as an International Language and Ph.D. in Education from University of Illinois (Urbana-Champaign), U.S. Her research interests include ELT methodology, materials development, and professional development. Dr. Park is the former president of the Pan-Korea English Teachers Association. She served as a visiting professor at Ritsumeikan University, Japan, Monash University, Australia, and Harvard University, U.S. She has given numerous presentations in Japan, Australia, Malaysia, India, Thailand, the Philippines, Singapore, Hong Kong, Vietnam, China, Russia, Indonesia, and Macao. She can be reached at mrpark@pknu.ac.kr.

Marine English

초판인쇄 2018년 11월 28일
초판발행 2018년 11월 28일

지은이 Mae-Ran Park
펴낸이 채종준
펴낸곳 한국학술정보(주)
주소 경기도 파주시 회동길 230(문발동)
전화 031) 908-3181(대표)
팩스 031) 908-3189
홈페이지 http://ebook.kstudy.com
전자우편 출판사업부 publish@kstudy.com
등록 제일산-115호(2000. 6. 19)

ISBN 978-89-268-8633-5 93330